The Algarve

DIRECTIONS

WRITTEN AND RESEARCHED BY

Matthew Hancock

WITH ADDITIONAL ACCOUNTS BY

Amanda Tomlin

NEW YORK • LONDON • DELHI
www.roughguides.com

Contents

Introduction to

The Algarve

With some of Europe's best sandy beaches, idyllic rocky coves, fresh seafood and picturesque fishing villages, the Algarve is justifiably the most popular region in Portugal for both overseas visitors and the Portuguese themselves. It's a year-round destination, with bright, mild winters and long, balmy summers; it's rare for the sun not to make an appearance even in midwinter, and a local Algarve saying maintains that "Saturday without sun is like Sunday without a church service".

At just 240km from east to west and 40km from north to south at its widest point, it is easy to take in the region's big sights in a relatively short space of time. There is a good network of roads, an efficient bus

▲ Praia de São Rafael

When to visit

Sunny, warm weather with barely a cloud in sight is pretty much guaranteed in high season (late May to early October); during this time most resorts are bustling. Peak season is in July and August, when you can expect temperatures of 25–30°C, though cooling Atlantic breezes usually make things comfortable.

Golfers ensure that autumn remains a busy season, as the cooler breezes off the coast in September and October are ideal for the game. But it is not too cool for beachgoers either, and swimming is tempting well into October (and year-round if you're hardy, with water temperatures rarely dropping below 15°C).

The region is perhaps at its best in spring or winter, with temperatures usually a pleasant 15–18°C, the countryside at its most lush and the resorts delightfully quiet. Despite the chance of the occasional downpour, most hotels and restaurants stay open, and many hotels offer generous discounts.

service and quaint railway line, making all places relatively accessible from the airport at Faro, the regional capital.

Popularity has led to heavy development on the central coastal strip from Faro west to Lagos. But even here you can find quiet cove beaches and vestiges of traditional Portugal amongst the panoply of villas, hotels and sports complexes. It is this combination of natural beauty and superb facilities that has made the region popular with celebrities and sports stars, from Cliff Richard and Madonna to a fair proportion of the England football team.

Development is much less pronounced at the two extremes of the Algarve. Around Sagres and along the west coast, low-key resorts are close to a series of breathtaking, wave-battered beaches, popular with surfers. To the east, relaxed resorts lie within reach of island sandbanks boasting giant swathes of dune-backed beaches. Away from the coast, inland Algarve has a surprisingly diverse landscape, with lush orange groves and wooded mountains offering superb

◄ Estói church

▲ Algarve crafts

walking territory around Monchique and Silves to the west and the Serra do Caldeirão in the centre. In the east, a more wildly beautiful landscape marks the border with Spain along the fertile Guadiana river valley.

The Algarve
AT A GLANCE

WEST OF FARO

The international airport is located near the regional capital Faro, a picturesque and historic harbour town. Within easy reach are the purpose-built resorts of Quinta do Lago, Vale de Lobo and Vilamoura, each with grand beaches, international restaurants and a brace of golf courses and sports facilities.

THE EASTERN ALGARVE

Characterful towns such as Olhão, Fuzeta and Tavira are just a short ride from some of the region's most spectacular beaches – although much of the eastern

Algarve is fronted by the Parque Natural da Ria Formosa, important wetlands protected by a series of six barrier islands.

◄ Spanish border village

▼ Tavira

THE SPANISH BORDER

The historic border town of Vila Real de Santo António gives easy access to Spain and sits on the verdant Guadiana river. This natural boundary with Spain is bolstered by impressive fortresses in the villages of Alcoutim and Castro Marim. West of here lies a wild mountainous landscape of small agricultural villages and spectacular scenery.

▲ Vau beach

THE CENTRAL ALGARVE

The central stretch of coast contains the classic postcard images of the province – tiny bays, broken up by rocky outcrops and fantastic grottoes, at their most exotic around the major resorts of Albufeira, Armação de Pêra and Carvoeiro. Here you'll find some of the region's biggest – if most developed – beaches at Galé, Praia da Rocha and Alvor.

INLAND

The inland Algarve is remarkably unspoilt, with picture-postcard villages such as Alte and Salir a world away from the coastal resorts. Here you'll find the Moorish capital Silves; the Serra de Monchique, the highest mountain range in the south, with great walks through the cork and chestnut woods; and a beautiful old spa village in Caldas de Monchique.

THE SOUTHWEST ALGARVE

The southwest Algarve embraces Lagos, one of the region's liveliest historic towns with some great beaches; and continues up to the cape at Sagres – once site of Henry the Navigator's naval school and the southwesternmost point of mainland Europe. In between, development is restricted to the area around the former fishing villages of Luz, Burgau and Salema, each with fine, cliff-backed beaches.

THE WEST COAST

Part of the Parque Natural do Sudoeste Alentejano e Costa Vicentina, the protected west coast shows a very different face of the Algarve. Cooler waters and crashing surf lie off the majestic beaches near Vila do Bispo, Carrapateira, Aljezur and Odeceixe. The area is thin on accommodation but very popular with surfers and lovers of unspoilt terrain.

▲ The Lagos coast

Ideas

The big six

Rightly famed for its stupendous beaches and year-round sunshine, the Algarve also boasts a diverse range of other attractions from whitewashed former fishing villages to ancient walled towns, and from wild mountain scenery to atmospheric wetlands. There's enough to keep visitors busy for weeks, though as the region is relatively small, you can see many of the following sights in just a few days.

▲ Albufeira

The region's most popular resort has a bit of everything: a superb town beach, a dazzling whitewashed old town, watersports and a nightlife where just about anything goes.

P.105 ▶ ALBUFEIRA AND AROUND

▲ Reserva Natural da Ria Formosa

Six unique barrier islands protecting a system of salt marshes and tidal mudflats, each fronted by sandspit beaches that spread as far as the eye can see.

P.78 & P.86 ▶ OLHÃO & WEST OF FARO

▶ Lagos

This attractive historic walled town sits within walking distance of pristine beaches and a sculpted coastline where boats can take you to visit rock pillars, blowholes and amazing grottoes.

▼ Serra de Monchique

Alluring footpaths and mountain roads criss-cross the beautiful wooded hills around Monchique, offering a peaceful alternative to the bustling beach resorts.

▶ Parque Natural da Costa Vicentina

The protected west coast of the Algarve is a surfers' paradise, a largely undiscovered stretch of wild coastline studded with exhilarating wave-battered beaches.

◀ Silves

Surrounded by orange groves, the former Moorish capital looks much as it has done for centuries, with a superb castle and historic cathedral.

Beaches

Few places in Europe have so many Blue Flag beaches in such a concentrated area. The east has enormous stretches of sand, many on offshore islets that can be reached by boat. The central region has more accessible sands, some sheltered by low cliffs. The west-coast beaches tend to be broad sandy bays onto which thunderous waves break. All beaches face the Atlantic, and though never as warm as the Med, it's never as cold out of season, and hardy swimmers take to the water all year round.

▲ Praia de Centianes

A spectacular beach hemmed in by dramatic cliffs, complete with a giant cave, ideal for escaping the midday heat.

P.118 ▶ ARMAÇÃO DE PERA AND AROUND

▼ Praia de Dona Ana

Perhaps the most photographed of the Algarve's beaches, this distinctive cove with its rock pillars and caves is best visited out of season, when it's much less crowded.

P.146 & P.150 ▶ LAGOS AND AROUND

▶ Ilha de Tavira

The most popular of the sandspit beaches, with some fourteen kilometres of soft sands that attract families and a young crowd.

P.86 ▶ TAVIRA AND AROUND

▲ Praia da Bordeira

No problems finding space on the giant swathe of sands here on the unspoilt west coast.

P.171 ▶ THE WEST COAST

▼ Sagres

Plenty of soft sands and watersports are to be found around the western town of Sagres.

P.164 ▶ SAGRES AND AROUND

▶ Praia da Marinha

Topped by a delightful coastal path, this is one of the least visited of the cliff-backed coves in the central Algarve.

P.118 ▶ ARMAÇÃO DE PERA AND AROUND

Historical Algarve

The Romans inevitably left their mark on the Algarve. However, it was the Moors – who occupied the region for around five hundred years until 1249 – who left a more lasting influence, introducing a new architectural style, farming techniques and *azulejos* (tiles). Many place names are derived from the Arabic, including the Algarve itself – from *al-Gharb*, "the west". In the fifteenth century, the Algarve's ports became the main departure points for the great Portuguese navigators, and their legacy can be seen in many of the region's churches and monuments.

▼ Vila Real

The Great Earthquake of 1755 did much to end Portugal's glory days. Vila Real was one of the towns that managed to rise from the ruins and became a symbol of post-quake Portugal. Its grid of streets were built using the same town planning techniques as had been used in Lisbon.

P.97 ▸ VILA REAL, THE GUADIANA AND THE SERRA DE ALCARIA

▼ Silves

Silves was one of Iberia's most important Moorish centres until 1189, when it was captured by Christians under Dom Sancho I, whose statue still guards the walls.

P.126 ▸ SILVES AND AROUND

▲ Milreu

The area's most important Roman site, complete with fish mosaics, a bath house and the remains of one of the earliest Christian churches in the world.

P.74 ▸ NORTH OF FARO

▶ Sagres

The instigator of the great maritime explorations, Henry the Navigator set up a School of Navigation at this windswept promontory in around 1420, opening up the unknown world to Portugal's traders.

P.164 ▸ SAGRES AND AROUND

◀ Vilamoura

Low-density, high-tech and stuffed with sports amenities, Vilamoura represents the future of the Algarve, a purpose-built resort catering to the tastes of the Euro zone.

P.64 ▸ WEST OF FARO

▶ Lagos

The country's first slave market appeared in Lagos in 1444. The trade ironically helped finance further maritime explorations and by the mid-sixteenth century, Portugal – along with Spain – dominated world trade, with trading posts from Macau in the east to Brazil in the west.

P.146 ▸ LAGOS AND AROUND

Best museums

Though none of the Algarve's museums can be described as unmissable, they do offer an insight into the culture, crafts and traditions that make the region so proud of its distinct identity. Many are set in buildings that are worth a visit in their own right, and entry fees rarely exceed €3. As elsewhere in Portugal, most museums close on Mondays.

▼ **Museu Arqueológico, Faro**

Housed in an ancient convent with one of the most beautiful cloisters in the country, Faro's main museum also displays Moorish lamps, Roman mosaics and some fine modern paintings.

P.53 ▶ FARO AND AROUND

▶ Museu Etnográfico do Trajo Algarvio, São Bras de Alportel

Neatly preserved agricultural equipment, a traditional well and historical costumes add up to one of the most engaging of the Algarve's cultural museums.

P.72 ▸ NORTH OF FARO

◀ Museu Regional, Lagos

A treasure trove-cum-junk shop of a museum, with everything from Roman busts to crafts and rusting surgical instruments.

P.149 ▸ LAGOS AND AROUND

▼ Museu Arqueológico, Silves

Partly set in the old town walls, Silves' archeological museum romps through Portugal's history with a diverse range of exhibits, including an intact ten-metre-deep Moorish well.

P.127 ▸ SILVES AND AROUND

▲ Museu Arqueológico, Loulé

Located within Loulé's castle, this tiny museum shows off the foundations of a Moorish house, re-creates a traditional kitchen and allows visitors access to the castle walls.

P.70 ▸ NORTH OF FARO

Castles

The Algarve has historically been vulnerable to attack, and fortifications became essential to protect the key settlements. Many of today's castles are adaptations of original Moorish structures; others were built in the thirteenth century during the reign of Dom Dinis, one of the country's first monarchs who saw the importance of strengthening his frontiers. Today, some castles function as museums, and most at least afford fine views and a tranquil retreat.

▲ Castro Marim

Facing the Spanish border, this thirteenth-century stronghold was the former headquarters of the Order of Christ, a chivalric order that protected Portugal's remote areas for the Church and king.

P.99 ▶ VILA REAL, GUADIANA AND THE SERRA DE ALCARIA

▼ Paderne

Apart from the nearby highway, Paderne's ruined Moorish castle sits in splendid rural isolation.

P.110 ▶ ALBUFEIRA AND AROUND

▼ Aljezur

The remains of the tenth-century Moorish castle quietly brood on a hilltop overlooking this pretty town in the western Algarve.

P.172 ▶ THE WEST COAST

▼ Silves

Silves castle dominates the town and is one of the most impressive fortifications in the region.

P.127 ▶ SILVES AND AROUND

▼ Ferragudo

Though not open to the public, Ferragudo's sixteenth-century Castelo de São João do Arade is one of the only castles in the region impressively sited right on the beach itself.

P.122 ▶ CARVOEIRO AND AROUND

Churches

Though the religious centre of Portugal is in Braga, in the north, the Catholic Church has been highly influential in the Algarve's development. Many churches date from the Golden Age of the sixteenth century, when funds were lavished on ornate, maritime-influenced carvings and Gothic-influenced architecture known as the Manueline style. Many of the churches withstood the devastating earthquake of 1755 and today remain some of the region's oldest and most rewarding places to visit, rich in architecture and *azulejos*.

▲ Igreja de Santo António, Lagos

This fantastically embellished, barrel-vaulted, eighteenth-century church is a masterpiece of Baroque architecture.

P.149 ▸ LAGOS AND AROUND

▲ Sé Velha, Faro

Faro's cathedral is the most important church in the Algarve, much of it dating from the thirteenth century.

P.52 ▸ FARO AND AROUND

▲ Nossa Senhora de Guadalupe

Tradition maintains that Henry the Navigator was a frequent visitor to this thirteenth-century church set in a lonely field.

P.159 ▶ THE SOUTH WEST COAST

▶ Igreja Matriz, Alvor

A sixteenth-century church embellished in the distinctive Manueline architectural style – all twisted pillars and ornate carved doors.

P.135 ▶ PORTIMÃO, PRAIA DA ROCHA AND AROUND

▼ Nossa Senhora Piedade, Loulé

One of the most distinctive of the region's modern churches and the central focus for the important Mãe Soberana Easter parade.

P.70 ▶ NORTH OF FARO

On the tiles

Decorative tiles – *azulejos* – can be seen both inside and outside houses, churches, cafés and even train stations. The craft was brought to Iberia by the Moors in the eighth century, the word deriving from the Arabic *al-zulecha*, "small stone". Changing technology and fashions have led to various styles of *azulejo* panels, including religious imagery, decorative tiled walls known as *tapetes* (rugs), Rococo designs, satirical portraits and contemporary designs.

▲ Hotel Bela Vista Praia da Rocha

This beautiful, early twentieth-century hotel displays the best in Portuguese interior decor.

P.137 ▶ PORTIMÃO, PRAIA DA ROCHA AND AROUND

▲ Bakery, Cabanas

Azulejos are as eye-catching as any street sign, as on this local bakery.

P.92 ▶ THE EASTERN ALGARVE

▶ Flats, Monte Gordo

Useful both for insulation and decoration,
tiles are still used on buildings to this day.

P.94 ▶ THE EASTERN ALGARVE

▲ Igreja de São Laurenço Almancil

The church's interior is lined with sumptuous
tiles depicting the life of Saint Lawrence,
painted in 1730 by one of the country's
leading artists.

P.61 ▶ WEST OF FARO

▼ Market, Quarteira

Tiles also show what's for sale in markets,
as here outside Quarteira market.

P.63 ▶ WEST OF FARO

Nature

The Algarve's wildlife varies from wild boar in the interior to rare wading birds on the coastal mudflats. Plant life is also abundant: carob, citrus and olive trees were introduced by the Moors, and some olive trees are believed to be up to one thousand years old. Almond trees contribute to many of the region's marzipan-based sweets, and blossom spectacularly in February, earning them the nickname "snow of the Algarve". Another prized species is the umbrella pine, which offers shade to many golf courses.

▲ Quinta da Rocha

This flat river estuary supports some 22 species of wading bird, such as the sanderling and knot.

P.135 ▸ PORTIMÃO, PRAIA ROCHA AND AROUND

▲ Cabo de São Vicente

Portugal's southwestern most point supports the highest proportion of marine and bird life in the country, including sea otters, Bonelli's eagles, ospreys, kites and white herons.

P.166 ▸ SAGRES AND AROUND

◀ São Bras de Alportel

Some fifty percent of the world's cork supplies come from southern Portugal, and the ancient cork groves around São Bras offer a habitat for wild boar, foxes and the extremely rare Iberian lynx.

P.72 ▸ NORTH OF FARO

▶ Reserva Natural do Sapal de Castro Marim

The marshy riverside reserve near the Spanish border is home to spoonbills, winter flamingos and the rare swivel-eyed Mediterranean chameleon, famed for its phenomenally long tongue.

P.100 ▸ VILA REAL, THE GUADIANA AND THE SERRA DE ALCARIA

▼ Parque Natural da Ria Formosa

One of the most important wetlands in Iberia, sheltering fish, reptiles and wading birds; the reserve's rarest species is the purple galinule, a stumpy, swamp-loving bird.

P.62 ▸ WEST OF FARO

Sport

The Algarve has some of Europe's best year-round sports facilities.

Famed for its golf, the region also has world-class tennis centres and well-equipped marinas. With its swell sizes of up to fifteen feet, Portugal is one of Europe's top surfing destinations (see pp.28–29), while windsurfing and kite surfing are also growing in popularity. You can see top soccer action at the futuristic Algarve stadium, and – though not something all tourists wish to support – bullfights take place in Albufeira.

▲ Golf

Some of the country's best golf courses are to be found in the region – a round at Pine Cliffs is always memorable.

P.185 ▸ ESSENTIALS

▲ Lisbon–Dakar Rally

The opening stages of the famous rally pass through the region, usually around Monchique in early January. Details on Ⓦwww.dakar.com.

P.141 ▸ SERRA DE MONCHIQUE

▲ Tennis

The Vale de Lobo Tennis Academy, run by ex-Portuguese pro Pedro Frazão, is frequented by Tim Henman and is the highest rated of the region's many tennis centres.

P.63 ▸ WEST OF FARO

▼ Windsurfing

With constant winds averaging force 3–5, the Algarve offers excellent windsurfing, with many windsurfing schools like this one at Praia da Martinhal.

P.166 ▸ SAGRES AND AROUND

▲ Cycling

With the new Ecovias cycle way (ⓦwww.ecoviasalgarve.org) crossing the entire region from Sagres to the east, it is easier than ever to explore the Algarve by bike.

P.180 ▸ ESSENTIALS

Surfing

Whatever the weather, you can nearly always be sure of excellent surfing conditions in the Algarve. The swell "wraps" round Cabo de São Vicente, producing relatively gentle waves in the bays between Sagres and Lagos, ideal for inexperienced surfers. More experienced surfers should head for the west coast where swell sizes reach up to 5m. If you're new to surfing you're best off going with a surf school – which can give one-off lessons or courses – or a surf camp, which throws in accommodation and transport to the best beaches.

▲ The west coast

There are several surf camps and surf schools along the west coast including ⓦwww.freeridesurfcamp.com, ⓦwww.algarvesurfschool.com, ⓦwww.surferdream.com/Algarve and ⓦwww.surf-experience.com.

P.171 ▸ THE WEST COAST

▼ Arrifana

Broad sands and big waves allure surfers to this beach below high cliffs.

P.172 ▸ THE WEST COAST

▲ Sagres

The region's surf "capital", with great beaches for beginners and experienced surfers.

P.164 ▸ SAGRES AND AROUND

◄ Praia do Amado

Legs of the World Surfing Championship are often held at this exposed west coast beach.

P.171 ▸ THE WEST COAST

▼ Praia de Tonel

"Tunnel beach" feels the brunt of the Atlantic breakers, making it the pick of Sagres' many beaches.

P.165 ▸ SAGRES AND AROUND

Kids' Algarve

With comfortable hotels, a range of villas and miles of beach, the Algarve is perfect for family holidays. The Portuguese are very family-oriented and children are welcomed everywhere – expect to see kids out in public squares and restaurants until midnight. There are also various attractions designed especially for children, including water parks, zoos and mini-train rides. Coin-operated rides also feature outside shops and cafés, while playgrounds are to be found all over the region.

▲ Zoo Marine

Part zoo, part theme park and wholly delightful for kids, with performing dolphins, sea lions, birds and various aquatic beasties.

P.109 ▸ ALBUFEIRA AND AROUND

▲ Krazy World

Another zoo-cum-theme park boasting fairground rides, animal parks, crazy golf and some fearsome snakes.

P.109 ▸ ALBUFEIRA AND AROUND

▲ Slide and Splash

The name says it all, as does the Kamikaze, one of several high-thrill water slides and chutes.

P.122 ▸ CARVOEIRO AND AROUND

▶ Pedras d'el Rei

Getting to the superb beach at Barril is half the fun: take the toy train from the holiday village of Pedras d'El Rei.

P.87 ▸ TAVIRA AND AROUND

▼ Lagos Zoo

Wallabies, monkeys, Vietnamese pigs and exotic birds roam this well laid-out zoo northwest of Lagos.

P.152 ▸ LAGOS AND AROUND

Shops and markets

Amongst the tourist souvenirs, you can still find traditional arts and crafts in the region's shops and markets. Distinctive ceramics, copperwork, hand-knitted chunky jumpers and wooden furniture are of good quality and usually good value. So, too, are local food and drink specialities, such as cheeses and almond-based sweets and wines. These can be best value at covered markets, to be found in all the main towns. Many towns also have a weekly gypsy market, superb places for atmosphere and the odd bargain garment. For shopping hours see p.187.

▲ Chic shopping, Faro

Faro's pedestrianized shopping streets offer the best in Portuguese chic, while the giant Fórum Algarve shopping centre contains some two hundred shops.

P.51 ▶ FARO AND AROUND

◀ Markets, Loulé

Visit on a Saturday morning, when the covered market is at its most animated and the gypsy market visits the edges of town.

P.69 ▶ NORTH OF FARO

▲ Ceramics workshops, Porches

Porches is famed for its distinctive majolica pottery, but you can also buy ceramics from all over Portugal.

P.117 ▶ ARMAÇÃO DE PERA AND AROUND

◀ Folding chairs, Monchique

These beautifully crafted and distinctive scissor chairs are typical of the region and make fine souvenirs.

P.141 ▶ SERRA DE MONCHIQUE

Boat trips

One of the best ways to appreciate the Algarve's dramatic coastal scenery is to take a boat trip. These range from hour-long cruises to full- or half-day excursions, often including a picnic lunch. Specialist fishing or dolphin-watching trips are also available. You can also explore inland, either on the waterways of the eastern Algarve or up the rivers Arade and Guadiana. The latter divides Portugal from Spain, and a boat trip across the border makes for a fun excursion.

▲ Up the Guadiana

Regular trips run from the border town of Vila Real pass up the Guadiana, with Spain on one side and Portugal on the other, through idyllic, unspoilt countryside.

P.101 ▶ VILA REAL, THE GUADIANA AND THE SERRA DE ALCARIA

▼ Lagos

Some of the region's most dramatic rock formations can be seen by boat off Ponta da Piedade, the headland jutting out beyond Lagos.

P.151 ▶ LAGOS AND AROUND

PARIS :61-AL

▲ Vilamoura

The marina offers countless boat trips – head up the coast past remote beaches and, if you are lucky, dolphins will follow in your wake.

P.64 ▸ WEST OF FARO

▼ Vila Real to Spain

The ferry to Spain is a delightful trip across the Guadiana to the picturesque border town of Ayamonte.

P.98 ▸ VILA REAL, GUADIANA AND THE SERRA DE ALCARIA

▶ Parque Natural da Ria Formosa

Safari boat trips like this one from Santa Luzia explore the important wetlands and beaches of the Parque Natural da Ria Formosa.

P.87 ▸ TAVIRA AND AROUND

Prettiest villages

Decades of tourism have left their mark on the region, and many of the former tranquil fishing villages are all but lost in a tangle of villa complexes. But there are still some settlements that have remained unscathed and highly picturesque, from atmospheric fishing villages to dazzling whitewashed mountain hamlets. Even these places get summer visitors, but go out of season or at the end of the day and they reveal what the Algarve was like a century ago.

▲ Caldas de Monchique

Avoid the midday coach parties and this tiny spa village located in chestnut woods in the Serra de Monchique is delightfully tranquil.

P.142 ▸ SERRA DE MONCHIQUE

▲ Cacela Velha

Overlooking its distant sandspit beach, this little clifftop town looks much as it must have for centuries.

P.92 ▸ THE EASTERN ALGARVE

▲ Salir

A traditional inland village set in rolling countryside and boasting the remains of a Moorish castle.

P.72 ▶ NORTH OF FARO

◀ Alte

Often billed as the prettiest village in the Algarve, Alte has dazzling white houses festooned with geraniums and is located near tranquil natural springs.

P.110 ▶ ALBUFEIRA AND AROUND

▼ Alcoutim

A picture-book border settlement with its own castle facing the River Guadiana and a mirror-image village over the border in Spain.

P.101 ▶ VILA REAL, THE GUADIANA AND THE SERRA DE ALCARIA

Festivals and events

Though superficially less exuberant than their Spanish neighbours, the Portuguese certainly know how to have a good time when it comes to festivals, and virtually every village in the Algarve has at least one of these at some stage of the year. Most revolve around celebrating the patron saint of the community, with a few pagan traditions thrown in for good measure. A church service is usually followed by a parade, music and dancing, with plenty of alcohol.

▲ 25 de Abril, Faro

Faro and other towns host parades, fireworks and live music to mark the day of Portugal's revolution in 1974.

P.51 ▸ FARO AND AROUND

▼ Mãe Soberana, Loulé

The region's most important religious festival, when an image of Our Lady of Piety is carried into town in an Easter procession.

P.70 ▸ NORTH OF FARO

▶ Sardine festival, Quarteira

Row upon row of sizzling bodies may be
nothing new on Quarteira's beaches, but in
August grilled sardines take centre stage,
with a massive set-up on the beach.

P.63 ▸ WEST OF FARO

◀ Festa de Santos Populares

June sees riotous street parties celebrating
the popular saints of António (12–13), João
(23–24) and Pedro (28–29); Tavira's Festa de
Santo António is one of the liveliest.

P.185 ▸ ESSENTIALS

▼ Almond blossom, Guadiana

The spectacular blossoming of the almond
trees in January and February is known as
the "snow of the Algarve" – according to
legend a Moorish king planted the trees in
order to placate his Swedish wife who pined
for the snows of winter.

P.101 ▸ VILA REAL, GUADIANA
AND THE SERRA DE
ALCARIA

▲ Beer Festival, Silves

Silves suddenly becomes a very popular
destination when international and local
beers are quaffed by the barrel, usually
in July.

P.128 ▸ SILVES AND AROUND

Food and drink

A plate of fresh sardines with a cool beer at sunset is one of the quintessential Portuguese beachside experiences, but there is more to the local cuisine than that. Much of Portugal's fantastic seafood comes from the Algarve, and you shouldn't miss the opportunity to sample its prawns, clams and unique seafood dishes. Fresh fish is generally affordable, varied and nearly always excellent, grilled meats are reliably tasty, while a decent local wine can be enjoyed at even the humblest of cafés.

▲ Wine

Inexpensive and drinkable, the Algarve's most famous wines come from Cliff Richard's wine estate, though wines from Estremadura, Ribatejo and the Douro are hard to fault.

P.111 ▶ ALBUFEIRA AND AROUND

▼ Cataplana

The delicious fish bouillabaisse-type dish takes its name from the copper pans that they are cooked in, a vessel dating back to Moorish times. *Quatro Águas* near Tavira does a superb one.

P.91 ▶ TAVIRA AND AROUND

▲ Sardines

The traditional Portuguese dish, *sardinhas no churrasco* (grilled sardines) are said to be best when there is no "r" in the month (ie May–Aug). Olhão market shows how fresh they can be.

P.77 ▸ OLHÃO AND AROUND

◀ Pastéis de Nata

The recipe for these custard tartlets has been Portugal's most successful export since Ronaldo. They are best enjoyed sprinkled with cinnamon and washed down with a coffee outside a café like *Gardy* in Faro.

P.58 ▸ FARO AND AROUND

▶ Presunto

Presunto – smoked ham – is one of the little-known delights of southern Portugal, and some of the best come from the mountains round Monchique. It even has its own ham festival in July.

P.141 ▸ SERRA DE MONCHIQUE

Cafés, bars and clubs

Portugal has a thriving café society and it is easy to fall into the local custom of punctuating the day with regular drink stops. Every town and resort has a fine range of café-bars, from Art Deco wonders with marble tabletops to flash steel-and-chrome designer buildings serving the latest cocktails. Most of the big resorts have at least one glitzy club, too; the majority get going at around midnight and keep going until the small hours.

▲ Anazu, Tavira

The perfect suntrap for a breakfast or evening drink, facing the Rio Gilão.

P.90 ▶ TAVIRA AND AROUND

▲ Café Inglês, Silves

An arty converted town house nestling on cobbled steps below Silves castle, with frequent exhibitions, along with fine food and drink.

P.130 ▶ SILVES AND AROUND

▲ Sete, Vilamoura

Part-owned by Luís Figo, this bar overlooking Vilamoura marina is perfect for star-spotting by day or night.

P.68 ▸ WEST OF FARO

◄ Rua Candido dos Reis, Albufeira

This narrow pedestrianized strip is lined with bars vying to outdo each other with the loudest music and most risqué-sounding cocktail.

P.105 ▸ ALBUFEIRA AND AROUND

▼ Café Calcina, Loulé

Tuck into a beer and *tremoços* (pickled lupin seeds) at Loulé's most atmospheric café.

P.75 ▸ NORTH OF FARO

Restaurants

Eating out at a restaurant is a popular pastime for most Portuguese, and restaurants are plentiful and inexpensive. Upmarket restaurants often grab the top locations, but you can still find affordable places right on the beachfronts. The atmospheric backstreets are where you'll often track down the liveliest local haunts, often with a TV in one corner, children running round until midnight and ample food.

▲ Rei das Praias, Praia de Caneiros

Top food in a great location, in a simple beach restaurant on the beach, makes a meal here a memorable occasion.

P.125 ▸ CARVOEIRO AND AROUND

▼ Caminé

Politicians and stars like to dine at this swish restaurant offering deluxe Portuguese cuisine facing a lagoon.

P.59 ▸ FARO AND AROUND

▲ Raposo

Enjoy fish, seafood and views at this great beachside restaurant.

P.169 ▶ SAGRES AND AROUND

▲ Dona Barca, Portimão

One of the region's most highly rated restaurants, with outside seats on a tranquil patio.

P.139 ▶ PORTIMÃO, PRAIA DA ROCHA AND AROUND

▲ A Ruina, Albufeira

This restaurant, serving superbly grilled fish, is partly set in the ruins of the old town walls, and tables are set out on the sands in summer.

P.114 ▶ ALBUFEIRA AND AROUND

Weird and wonderful

Some of the Algarve's charm lies in the unexpected sights that you come across when exploring the region – from ragged storks' nests that cap the chimneys and church towers in early summer to remote hamlets where women still wear traditional dress, and from farmers tilling their fields with mules to schools of dolphins suddenly rising out of the waves.

▲ Votive offerings, Olhão

It is traditional to leave wax or plastic body parts in churches, as at the church of Nossa Senhora do Rosário in Olhão shown here, in order to obtain a blessing to cure ailments.

P.76 ▶ OLHÃO AND AROUND

▼ Rosa dos Ventos, Sagres

This extraordinary wind compass, used to measure the wind direction, may date back to the time of Henry the Navigator.

P.164 ▶ SAGRES AND AROUND

▲ Capela dos Ossos, Faro

One way to line your walls – this bizarre chapel is completely decorated with human bones.

P.54 ▶ FARO AND AROUND

▲ Aquatic poodles, Quinta da Marim

It may sound like a shaggy dog story, but these aquatic dogs really were bred to help chase fish into fishermen's nets.

P.79 ▶ OLHÃO AND AROUND

▶ The lighthouse, Cabo de São Vicente

Marking what was once considered the edge of the world, this lighthouse has the most powerful beam in Europe.

P.166 ▶ SAGRES AND AROUND

Places

Faro and around

With its international airport, impressive shopping centre and ring of high-rise apartments, Faro boasts something of a big-city feel. The central area, however, is both attractive and manageable, and its harbourside gardens, semi-walled old town and range of shops make it a fine place to start or finish a tour of the region. It has been the administrative capital of the Algarve since 1776. The Romans, Moors and Spanish all ruled for a time, though today's mosaic-paved pedestrianized streets around Rua de Santo António are decidedly Portuguese in character, filled with aromatic cafés, restaurants and shops. Faro is cut off from the sea by a marshy lagoon, but lies within easy reach of two fine sandspit beaches, as well as the impressive Algarve stadium.

The harbour and marina

Embracing a small marina, the harbour is Faro's natural focus: the town gardens and a cluster of outdoor cafés overlook the rows of sleek yachts, and, at the end of the day, much of Faro gathers to promenade here. To the north there's a small **Museu Marítimo** (Mon–Fri 2.30–4.30pm; free), a modest maritime museum with engaging displays of model boats and local fishing techniques. From the leafy Jardim Manuel Bivar the **Comboio Turístico**

▼ FARO MARINA

train (hourly 10am–midnight; €3) starts its circuit of the town, trundling up past the Sé and through the modern town before returning to the marina via the market.

South of the harbour, you can follow the railway line for an attractive walk along the seafront, with the town walls on one side and the mud flats on the other; a small arch through the old town walls offers an

Visiting Faro

The bus terminal is located on Avenida da República, just north of the harbour. The train station faces Largo da Estação, a couple of minutes further northwest. For details of arriving at Faro's modern international airport, see p.179.

Faro's main turismo is close to the harbourfront at Rua da Misericórdia 8 (daily: May–Sept 9.30am–7pm, closed 12.30–2pm Fri–Mon; Oct–April 9.30am–5.30pm, closed 1–2pm Fri–Mon; ☎ 289 803 604). The regional tourist office – Região de Turismo do Algarve – north of the old town at Avenida 5º Outubro (Mon–Fri 9.30am–12.30pm & 2–5.30pm; ☎ 289 800 400, ⓦ www.visitalgarve.pt) is another good source of information on the area as a whole.

approach to the Cidade Velha (see below). From the jetty opposite here, ferries depart for the local sandspit beaches (see p.55).

Cidade Velha

The oldest and most picturesque part of Faro, the Cidade Velha (old town), or Vila-Adentro ("town within"), is an oval of cobbled streets and whitewashed buildings set within sturdy town walls, parts of which you can climb for great views over the town. The most striking entrance to the old town is through the nineteenth-century town gate, the Arco da Vila, next to the turismo. The Neoclassical arch, often capped by a stork's nest, was built by the Italian architect Francisco Xavier Fabri, on a commission by the Algarve's bishop, Francisco Gomes do Avelar, whose memorial sits in an alcove inside the arch. From here, Rua do Município leads up to the majestic main square, Largo da Sé, lined with orange trees and flanked by the cathedral and a group of palaces – including the former bishop's palace. The **Sé** (cathedral; Mon–Sat 10am–6pm, Oct–April till 5pm, Sun open for Mass at 10am & noon; €2.50) itself is a squat, white mismatch of Gothic, Renaissance and Baroque styles, all heavily remodelled after the 1755 earthquake. It's worth looking inside for the fine eighteenth-century *azulejos*, though the main appeal is its clock tower, which you can climb up for superb views over the surrounding coastland.

▼ FARO'S CIDADE VELHA

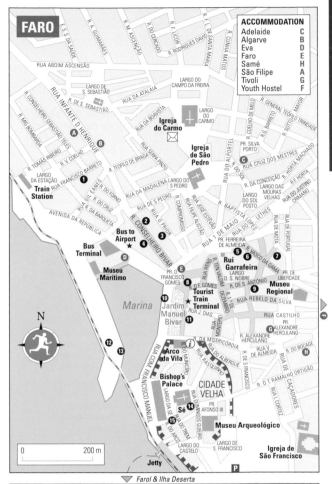

EATING & DRINKING

Adega Dois Irmãos	6	Conselheiro	2	Mesa dos Mouros	15
Adega Nova	1	Coreto	10	Millenium III	3
Aliança	8	Faro e Benfica	13	Sol e Jardim	5
Clube Naval	12	Gardy	9	Taberna da Sé	14
Columbus	11	Gengibre Canela	7	Upa Upa	4

Museu Arqueológico

Praça Afonso III. June–Sept Tues–Fri 10am–7pm, Sat & Sun 11.30am–6pm; Oct–May Tues–Fri 10am–6pm, Sat & Sun 10am–5pm. €2. Housed in the sixteenth-century Convento de Nossa Senhora da Assunção, which has one of the most beautiful cloisters in the country, the Museu Arqueológico is the Algarve's oldest museum, opened in 1894. The most striking of the museum's exhibits is a superb

▲ LARGO DA SÉ

Francisco, rebuilt in the eighteenth century on the site of an earlier church. Plain on the outside, the interior contains Baroque tiles and beautiful Rococo woodwork.

Igreja do Carmo and Igreja de São Pedro

Largo do Carmo. Mon–Fri 10am–1pm & 3–6pm (until 5pm Oct–April), Sat 10am–1pm, Sun only for Mass at 9am. By far the most curious sight in town lies in the twin-towered, Baroque **Igreja do Carmo**. A door to the right of the altar leads to the sacristy where you can buy a ticket for the macabre Capela dos Ossos (Chapel of Bones; €1.50), set in an attractive garden. Like the one at Alcantarilha (see p.117), its walls are decorated with human bones as a reminder of mortality – in this case disinterred in the nineteenth century from the adjacent monks' cemetery.

Nearby, on Largo de São Pedro, the sixteenth-century Igreja de São Pedro is one of the town's most attractive churches, with a finely decorated altar (to the left of the main altar), whose central image is a gilded, wooden Last Supper.

Museu Regional

Praça de Liberdade 2. Mon–Fri 9am–noon & 2–5pm. €1.50. One of the most likeable of Faro's museums, the Museu Regional displays local crafts and industries, including reconstructions of cottage interiors and models of the net systems still used for tuna fishing. There are also black-and-white photos of the

fourth-century AD Roman mosaic of Neptune surrounded by the four winds, unearthed near the train station. Other items include a fine collection of Roman statues from the excavations at Estói (see p.74), exquisite Moorish lamps, vases and bowls, and Baroque and Renaissance paintings from the sixteenth to nineteenth centuries. More modern are the futurist works of art by Carlos Porfírio, one of the country's leading twentieth-century painters.

Largo de São Francisco

South of the Cidade Velha and marked by an impressive fountain, the wide Largo de São Francisco serves as a giant car park for most of the year, but is cleared in late October for the Feira de Santa Iria, an enormous market-cum-fairground with live entertainment over the best part of a week. The square is overlooked by the **Igreja da Ordeu Terceira de São**

town and local beaches before tourism took hold.

Ilha Deserta and Ilha da Culatra

Ferries shuttle from Faro's jetty, just south of the harbour by the town wall, through narrow, marshy channels to the so-called **Ilha Deserta** (details on ☎289 806 840; June to mid-Sept 4 daily; €12 return), officially known as the Ilha da Barreta, part of the Parque Natural da Ria Formosa and the southernmost point of mainland Portugal. The sandspit island has a superb beach, though the name is a bit of a misnomer, as you'll have plenty of sun-worshippers for company and there is a pricey café, *O Estaminé*. Alternatively, there are guided trips, which run all year and include commentary on the local bird life (twice daily at 11am and 3pm, lasting 2hr 30min; €20 per person). Ferries also depart from the same jetty to Farol (see p.77) on the **Ilha da Culatra** (details on ☎917 634 813; June to mid-Sept 4 daily, first boat 9.30am, last return 7pm; €4 return).

Praia de Faro

Buses #14 and #16 from Faro's harbour gardens go via the bus station and airport (daily 7.10am–9pm, 8pm at weekends, every 45min; €1.50), terminating just before the narrow bridge to the beach. There are timetables posted at the bus stops; buy tickets on board. Lying just 3km from the airport, Praia de Faro makes a good base for a first or last night in the country. It is typical of the sandspit *ilha* beaches of the eastern Algarve: a long sweep of beautiful sand with both a sea-facing and a more sheltered lagoon-facing side. But being so near both the airport and Faro, it is inevitably overdeveloped, with bars, restaurants and villas jammed onto a sandy island almost too narrow to cope in the height of summer. Out of season, however, you'll probably have the sands to yourself. For more solitude, simply head west along the Praia de Faro towards Quinta do Lago (see p.62), where after 1km or so the crowds thin out. In July, the approaches to the beach host the annual Faro Bike Concentration (ⓦwww .motoclubefaro.pt), Europe's largest meeting of bikers, with plenty of live entertainment – the likes of Nazareth and Peter Frampton have appeared in recent years.

▼ THE BRIDGE TO PRAIA DE FARO

▲ ALGARVE STADIUM

Algarve stadium

Parque das Cidades ⓦ www
.parquecidades-eim.pt. Special bus
service for international matches,
concerts and events. Some 6km
north of Faro, between the main
Faro–Loulé road and the A22
motorway, the futuristic Algarve
sports stadium resembles an
open seashell, purpose-built as
the main southern venue for
Euro 2004. The 30,000 all-seater
stadium is the centrepiece of a
new cultural, sports and medical
park; along with sports events, it
hosts big-name concerts and the
Summer Festival in June, which
has lured Lenny Kravitz and Da
Weasel in recent years.

Accommodation

Residencial Adelaide

Rua Cruz das Mestres 7–9 ☎ 289 802
383, 🖷 289 826 870. The friendly
owner offers the best-value
accommodation in town, with
spotless en-suite rooms, cable
TV and an airy breakfast room.
Some rooms sleep 3–4. €50.

Estalagem Aeromar

Avda Nascente 1, Praia de Faro
☎ 289 817 542, ⓦ www.aeromar
.net. Right by the bridge over

to the sandspit, this is a good
choice if you've got an early
flight the next day. Set above
a decent restaurant, it offers
clean, comfortable rooms, some
with small balconies with views
either over the beach
(€8 extra) or of the planes
taking off across the inner
harbour. €82.

Residencial Algarve

Rua Infante Dom Henrique 52 ☎ 289
895 700, ⓦ residencialalgarve
.com. A modern *residencial* built
in traditional style. The spruce
rooms have spotless bathrooms
and cable TV, and breakfast
is served in a little patio in
summer. It's best to book ahead
as it is very popular. Front-
facing rooms can be noisy. €70.

Hotel Eva

Avda da República 1 ☎ 289 001 000,
ⓦ tdhotels.pt. This large, modern
block is the town's biggest
hotel, occupying a superb
harbourfront position. The
rooms are slightly worn, most
with balconies overlooking
the old town or the marina
(though the cheapest overlook
the bus station). There's a
decent top-floor restaurant,
small rooftop pool and a
courtesy bus to the local beach.
Disabled access. €145.

Hotel Faro

Praça Dr. Francisco Gomes 2 ☎ 289
830 830, ⓦ hotelfaro.pt. A modern
four-star facing the marina.
Rooms are functional and
geared to business travellers,
with mini-bar, cable TV and
a/c. Avoid those at the back
on the lower floors and opt
for the top ones facing the
marina. The main attraction is
the sunny roof terrace with its
own bar-restaurant with fine
views. €145.

Residencial Samé

Rua do Bocage 66 ☏ 289 824 375, ☏ 289 804 166. A slightly ageing hotel in a modern block with small but clean rooms just outside the old town. Some have balconies and all come with bathrooms and TV. There's an appealing communal lounge downstairs. €70.

Pensão São Filipe

Rua Infante Dom Henrique 55 ☏ 289 824 182, ⓦ guesthouse-saofilipe .com. Pristine rooms, with high ceilings, fans, cable TV and en-suite facilities. Avoid the front rooms that contend with the traffic of a busy through road. No breakfast. €55.

Pensão Tivoli Faro

Praça Alexandre Herculano 6 ☏ 289 829 825, ⓦ pension-tivoli .net. A welcoming English-run pension with a mixed bag of chracterful if noisy rooms with high ceilings and cable TV. Some have showers and small balconies, and you can use a communal kitchen and lovely roof terrace. No breakfast. €40.

Youth hostel

Rua da Policia de Segurança Pública (PSP) ☏ & ☏ 289 826 521. Faro's youth hostel is located in a quiet spot to the north of the old town, near attractive public gardens. Prices are €13 for beds in dorms of four to eight people, or €30 for a double room, €38 en-suite. Disabled access and use of communal kitchen.

Shops

Fórum Algarve

Daily 10am–11pm. A well-designed shopping centre clearly signed on the way to the airport, built round a fountain-filled central courtyard. Along with a multiplex cinema and various fast-food outlets, there are international stores such as Zara, Benetton, Pierre Cardin and Massimo Dutti, plus local favourites such as Sportzone and a Jumbo supermarket (closed Sun).

Rui Garrafeira

Praça Ferreira de Almeida 28. Mon–Sat 8am–8pm. A sumptuous

▲ RUA DE SANTO ANTÓNIO, FARO

deli-cum-off licence selling ports and wines to suit all budgets. This is also a good place to buy some of the excellent local cheeses, as well as chocolates and confectionery.

Cafés

Café Aliança
Rua Dr. Francisco Gomes 6–11. Mon–Sat 8am–midnight. This faded 1908 coffee house is said to be the oldest in Portugal, though the decor dates from the 1920s. Once the favoured haunt of the literary set, including Simone de Beauvoir, Fernando Pessoa and Mário Sá Carneiro, it remains wonderfully atmospheric. There are tables outside, and a full menu of inexpensive salads, omelettes, pastries and ice cream.

Café do Coreto
Jardim Manuel Bivar. Daily 8am–midnight. Glass-kiosk café-bar with prime seating facing the marina, a fine place to enjoy anything from breakfast and coffee to slightly pricey salads, sandwiches, ice creams and beers.

Gardy
Rua de Santo António 16. Mon–Fri & Sun 8.30am–11pm. A cavernous and popular local *pastelaria* with a counter piled high with cakes and savouries. Tables spilling out onto the main pedestrianized street and a side alley make this one of the best places in town to watch the world go by.

Restaurants

Adega Dois Irmãos
Largo Terreiro do Bispo 13–15 ☎289 823 337. Daily noon–4pm & 5.30–11pm. Opened in 1925 by two brothers (*irmãos*) in a former welder's shop, this tiled place is one of the oldest of the city's fish restaurants, with a little garden too. The day's catch can be expensive (around €15), though the *pratos de dia* are usually better value. Despite the number of tourists

▲ CAFÉ ALIANÇA

passing through, service remains courteous and efficient.

Adega Nova

Rua Francisco Barreto 24 ☎289 813 433. Daily noon–11pm. This great barn of a place is an old-fashioned *adega* with Portuguese food and jugs of wine. Turn up early, as the benches get packed, especially at weekends. There are a few vegetarian dishes and a kids' menu, and mains start at around €6. The adventurous can try *bife na pedra*: slices of beef that you cook at your table on a sizzling stone.

Caminé

Praia de Faro ☎289 817 539. Tues–Sun 12.30–3.30pm & 8–11pm. Just east of the main entrance to the beach and facing the inner harbour, this low glass-fronted restaurant is rated one of the Algarve's top restaurants and boasts the King of Spain and footballer Ruud Gullit as former guests. Dishes include *lagosta* (lobster), *fondue de tamboril e gambas* (monkfish and prawn fondue), *cataplana* and *caldeirada*. Expect to pay over €30 a head.

Clube Naval

Doca de Faro ☎289 823 869. Tues–Sun noon–3pm & 7–11pm. On a raised terrace right on the harbour, this is one of the few places in town where you can dine on moderately priced fish and grilled meats with fine views over the mud flats (and airport runway). Good-value shellfish and rice dishes start from €10, and you can get a superb *cataplana* for two at around €20.

Faro e Benfica

Doca de Faro ☎289 821 422. Mon & Wed–Sun 10.30am–2am. Closed

Nov. One of the best choices in town for a splurge on fish and seafood: specialities include *cataplanas*, oysters, crabs and lobster. Tables face the town across the harbour. Mains from around €18.

Gengibre Canela

Rua de Mota 10 ☎289 822 424. Mon–Sat noon–2.30pm. A small, cosy vegetarian restaurant, open for lunches only and serving good-value dishes along with salads and great fruit juices. There are a few outdoor tables on the street, too.

Mesa dos Mouros

Largo de Sé 10 ☎289 878 873. Tues–Sat 12.30–3pm & 7.30–10.30pm, Mon 7.30–10.30pm. A tiny, upmarket place – so it's best to book – serving cakes, drinks and refined cuisine including seafood and tasty chickpea salads. A few outdoor tables sit on the broad Largo de Sé itself.

Restaurante Paquete

Praia de Faro ☎289 817 760. May–Sept daily 10am–10pm; Oct–April Tues–Sun 10am–8pm. One of the beach's best-positioned café-restaurants, just west of the bridge that leads to the beach, with a sunny terrace facing the waves. It offers everything from giant toasted sandwiches and salads to decent, full and moderately priced Portuguese meals.

Sol e Jardim

Praça Ferreira de Almeida 22–23 ☎289 820 030. Mon–Sat 12.30–3pm & 7–11pm. Standard mid-priced Portuguese grills are served in this characterful restaurant with a barn-like "garden" dining room. Live folk music on Fridays adds to the fun.

Bars and clubs

Columbus

Jardim Manuel Bivar, corner with Rua João Dias ☎289 813 051. Tues–Sun 11am–1am. A jazzy local haunt with seats outside under the arcades opposite the harbourfront gardens. Take care on the dartboard if you've been downing the lethal sangrias and caipirinhas.

Conselheiro

Rua Conselheiro Bivar 72–78 ☎289 803 191. Daily 10pm–4am. A vibrant music bar with a large bar area, two dance floors, snooker room and videos; karaoke and Latin theme nights sometimes feature.

Millenium III

Rua do Prior 21 ☎289 823 628. Wed–Sat midnight–6am. Faro's main club, a large warehouse playing dance and Latin sounds. Look for flyers billing the latest guest DJs or visiting bands.

Taberna da Sé

Largo da Sé 26 ☎965 827 662. Mon–Sat 10am–midnight. An arty tavern in the old town with outdoor tables attracting a friendly, young crowd. It's a popular spot for spontaneous jamming sessions on a summer's evening.

Upa Upa

Rua Conselheiro Bivar 51 ☎289 807 832. Daily 9pm–4am, closed Sun Oct–April. A laid-back and relatively early-opening music bar with a mixed clientele and tables outside on the pedestrianized street.

West of Faro

West beyond Faro's international airport lie the very exclusive resorts of Quinta do Lago and Vale do Lobo. Studded with top golf courses and luxurious accommodation set amid neatly tended semi-tropical gardens, this is where the likes of Michael Owen and Madonna choose to holiday. Discreet low-density villa complexes are served by a plethora of sports facilities and restaurants, though in an area where flash cars are the norm, there's little in the way of public transport. Indeed, access to the area is a barely marked side-road from Almancil, whose church of São Laurenço has one of the most beautiful interiors in the country. Public transport improves around Vilamoura, a purpose-built international resort, fronted by a superb beach that stretches west to the former fishing village of Olhas d'Água. Quarteira is the only town on this stretch that is unashamedly downmarket, with a fine beach and bustling market.

Almancil and the Igreja de São Laurenço

Regular buses from Faro throughout the day. On the eastern edge of the rather unremarkable town of Almancil lies a hidden gem, the church of São Laurenço (Tues–Sat 10am–1pm & 2.30–5pm; €2). Built in the early eighteenth century, the church survived the earthquake of 1755 and retains its superb, fully tiled interior depicting the life of São Laurenço (St Lawrence), in particular, panels of his

▲ DETAIL, IGREJA DE SÃO LAURENÇO

martyrdom showing his death in graphic detail. They were painted in 1730 by Policarpo de Oliveira Bernardes, considered one of the country's best artists.

▼ IGREJA DE SÃO LAURENÇO, ALMANCIL

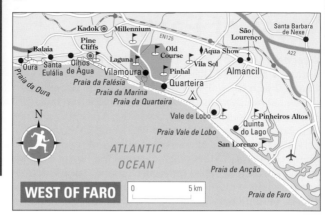

WEST OF FARO | 0   5 km

Quinta do Lago

Served by 1–2 daily buses from Loulé and Almancil. Fronted by a great beach and set amongst rolling grassland, waterways and pine forest, Quinta do Lago is Portugal's most upmarket purpose-built resort. A sprawling, luxury holiday village linked by miles of roads and roundabouts, it boasts top-class golf courses (see p.185), a watersports complex, riding centre and opulent hotels. The main car park is at the end of Avenida André Jorge, the main drag, from where a long wooden bridge crosses the Ria Formosa and dunes to the huge, splendid sandspit beach, a continuation of Praia de Faro (see p.55). The area around the wooden bridge gets packed in high season, but just

walk for ten minutes or so in either direction and you'll find plenty of empty sand.

The sandspit also protects the eastern extremity of the **Parque Natural da Ria Formosa**, an important wetland area for birds and wildlife. Two well-used nature trails are signed from next to the bridge. The longer and marginally more appealing one, the São Laurenço *trilho*, is an easy-to-follow 3.3-kilometre return walk southeast past bird hides to a Roman pillar. The shorter 2.3-kilometre return walk, the Quinta do Lago *trilho*, heads northwest to a small lake where flamingos sometimes feed. The freshwater lagoon at Ludo just to the east is one of the few places in Portugal where you can see the purple galinule, one of the country's rarest species of bird.

As you enter Quinta do Lago – at Roundabout 2 – there's a property sales office-cum-information centre (Mon–Fri 9.30am–1pm & 2.30–6pm; ☎289 351 900, ⓦwww .quintadolago.com), which can supply maps of the area.

▼ BRIDGE TO THE BEACH, QUINTA DO LAGO

Vale do Lobo

Served by 2 daily buses from Almancil.
Vale do Lobo means "Valley of
the Wolves", though there is little
wildlife left here. The resort is
similar to Quinta do Lago, with
serious-money hotels and low-
density upmarket villas. There is
a 24-hour reception as you enter
the complex (☎289 353 000,
Ⓦwww.valedolobo.com), which
can help with booking villas.
Vale do Lobo is something of a
prototype village which has won
a Green Globe award, a tourist
industry prize for environmental
awareness. The beach, Praia de
Vale do Lobo, is a magnificent
stretch of safe, soft sands with
plenty of beach paraphernalia
(sun loungers, umbrellas, etc) for
hire. First-rate sports facilities
include nearby golf courses (see
p.185) and the **Vale do Lobo
Tennis Academy** (☎289 357
850, Ⓦwww.premier-sports.org),
the most famous in the country,
frequented by the likes of Tim
Henman; as you'd expect, courts
get booked well in advance.

Quarteira

Quarteira has a very different
feel to the deluxe resorts either
side of it. It was one of the
first former fishing villages to
be developed in the Algarve, and
remains high-rise and
downmarket. Stick to the palm-
lined seafront promenade and
the attractive stretch of beach
– Praia de Quarteira – and it's
a pleasant enough destination,
although a little way inland
you're surrounded by rows of
tower blocks. The town remains
Portuguese in character, and
there's a good weekly market
each Wednesday – a section east
of the bus station sells clothes,
flowers and crafts. At other
times, the town's main attraction
is the bustling fish and vegetable
markets (daily 7am–3/4pm,
Oct–March closed Sun), by the
working fishing harbour to the
west end of town.

From May to September you
can tour Quarteira on a **toy
train** that trundles along the
seafront and round the town

ACCOMMODATION		EATING & DRINKING	
Dom José	C	Beira Mar	2
Miramar	B	O Jacinto	1
Romeu	A	Rosa Branca	3

▲ SEAFRONT, QUARTEIRA

every hour or so (daily 10am–midnight; €4).

Aqua Show

ⓦ aquashowpark.com. April–Oct daily 10am–5.30pm. €18, children under 12 €10. Around 5km inland from Quarteira, on the road to Loulé at Quatro Estradas, the **Aqua Show** water park makes a fun excursion, especially for kids, with various water chutes, pools, tropical birds and Europe's largest "watercoaster".

Vilamoura

Regular buses from Faro, Quarteira and Albufeira stop next to the casino one block from the Praia da Marina, where there's plenty of car-parking space. A short walk up the beach from Quarteira, based around Europe's largest marina, stands Vilamoura, a modern and constantly expanding resort, with a bewildering network of almost 200km of roads. The resort was created in the 1970s as an upmarket extension of Quarteira, with around one hundred restaurants and shops and a few appealing trails over its red-sand cliffs for walking and cycling. Beyond the marina, the development radiates outwards in a series of low-density hotels and over a thousand villas set in subtropical grounds amongst top-notch golf courses.

Bristling with high-tech powerboats and sleek yachts, the marina is the focus of the resort and is surrounded by international cafés, bars and restaurants. At the northwest end, various stalls offer **boat trips**, ranging from dolphin-watching excursions to fishing trips and parascending; prices start from around €15 for a two-hour trip to €50 for a full-day excursion. The boat trips are a great way to see the cliffs, coves and beaches of the surrounding coastline.

East of the marina, the stunning Praia da Marina has over 3km of soft, Blue Flag sands, though the crowds can be overwhelming in high season.

It might be hard to imagine today, but Vilamoura is an ancient settlement, and its history is traced in the **Museu Cerra da Vila** (daily 9.30am–12.30pm & 2–6pm;

Visiting Quarteira

The bus terminus (☏ 289 389 143) is a couple of blocks back from the beach, on Avenida Dr. Sá Carneiro, with the turismo on Praça do Mar by the beach (May–Sept Tues–Thurs 9.30am–7pm, Fri–Mon 9.30am–12.30pm & 2–6pm; Oct–April Tues–Thurs 9.30am–5.30pm, Fri–Mon 9.30am–1pm & 2–5.30pm; ☏ 289 389 209).

▲ VILAMOURA MARINA

€2), an important archeological site displaying the vestiges of a late Roman, Visigothic and Moorish colony. You can make out the foundations of a Roman mansion, baths and a fish-salting tank, together with well-preserved Roman mosaics. There's also a small exhibition hall with information about the history of the site.

Praia da Falésia

Praia da Falésia, a handsome stretch of sands backed by ochre-red sandstone cliffs (*falésias*) that give the beach its name, begins just west of Vilamoura marina. Getting there involves a short walk via a wooden footbridge over an inlet, so it's correspondingly less busy than Praia da Marina. Many of the dunes and cliffs here are part of the Parque Ambiental de Vilamoura, which has protected the beachside from the fairly uncontrolled development just back from the cliffs that stretches virtually all the way to Albufeira.

One of the most appealing of the region's trails begins at the edge of Vilamoura's beach car park, climbing the low, eroded cliffs, past spiky cactus plants, before rejoining the sands at the so-called Praia dos Tomates (Tomato Beach), where there is a seasonal café. Allow an hour for the full circuit.

Olhos de Água and Santa Eulalia

Served by regular bus from Albufeira. Olhos de Água, which translates as "eyes of the water", gets its name from the freshwater springs that bubble up under the sands. Its beach is broad, clean and alluring, though the once tiny fishing village is now all but engulfed by villas and restaurants tumbling down the steep slope to the coast.

At low tide you can walk the 2.5km from Olhos de Água along the beach to Praia da Oura, just 2km from Albufeira (see p.105). En route you pass Santa Eulalia, another fine beach dominated by a spa and hotel complex.

▲ PRAIA DA FALÉSIA

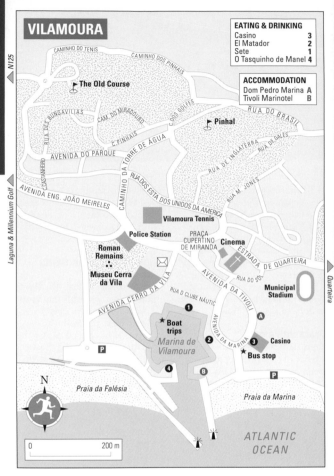

VILAMOURA

EATING & DRINKING
Casino	3
El Matador	2
Sete	1
O Tasquinho de Manel	4

ACCOMMODATION
| Dom Pedro Marina | A |
| Tivoli Marinotel | B |

CAMINHO DO TENIS
CAMINHO DOS PINHAIS
The Old Course
RUA DO BRASIL
RUA DAS BUNGAVILIAS
CAM. DO MIRADOURO
C. PINHAIS
C. DOS GOLFES
Pinhal
AVENIDA DO PARQUE
RUA DE INGLATERRA
RUA DE GALES
CASTANHEIRO
CAMINHO DA TORRE DE ÁGUA
RUA DOS ESTA DOS UNIDOS DA AMERICA
RUA M. JONES
AVENIDA ENG. JOÃO MEIRELES
Vilamoura Tennis
Police Station
PRAÇA CUPERTINO DE MIRANDA
Cinema
ESTRADA DE QUARTEIRA
Roman Remains
Museu Cerra da Vila
AVENIDA CERRO DA VILA
RUA D CLUBE NÁUTIC
AVENIDA DA TIVOLI
RUA DO SOL
Municipal Stadium
❶
Boat trips
Marina de Vilamoura
AVENIDA DA MARINA
❷
❸ Casino
Bus stop
A
❹
B
P
N
Praia da Falésia
Praia da Marina
P
ATLANTIC OCEAN
0   200 m

Accommodation

Hotel Dom José

Avda Infance de Sagres 143, Quarteira
☎289 310 210, ⓦwww.domjose
-hotels.com. A high-rise, fairly
characterless three-star hotel
right on the seafront that's
very popular with package
companies. The rooms are
decently sized with satellite TV
and a/c, and there's an in-house
pool, bar and restaurant. €120;
sea-view rooms cost €20 extra.

Dom Pedro Marina

Avda Tivoli, Vilamoura ☎289 381
100, ⓦwww.dompedro.com.
This triangular-shaped pink
block offers four-star facilities
including a pool and restaurant.
The best rooms have sea-facing
terraces (€40 extra), while the
presidential suites boast Jacuzzis
on their balconies. The less

expensive rooms overlook a car park. €240.

Le Meridien Dona Filipa

Vale do Lobo ☎289 357 200, ⓦwww .starwoodhotels.com. A five-star hotel near the beach set in luxuriant landscaped grounds with tennis courts. As you'd expect, rooms are sumptuous and expansive. There are also restaurants, a children's club and special family activities in summer. €300.

Pensão Miramar

Rua Gonçalo Velho 8, Quarteira ☎289 315 225, ⓕ289 314 671. Just off the seafront, this is much the best budget choice in town. The rooms are plain but spotless, with private bathrooms and TVs. Some have sea views, others face a charming internal terrace. There's also a great communal roof terrace. €70.

Hotel Quinta do Lago

Quinta do Lago ☎289 350 350, ⓦwww.quintadolagohotel.com. One of the country's top hotels, popular with celebrities who appreciate the privacy offered by its sprawling wooded grounds. Along with luxurious rooms, there are restaurants, bars, an indoor and outdoor pool, spa and sports facilities and discounts at the local golf courses. There are also eighteen family rooms. €440.

Pensão Romeu

Rua Gonçalo Velho 38, Quarteira ☎289 314 114. A friendly and very clean place, just up the road from the *Miramar* and almost identical in terms of its rooms and layout, though it lacks the sea views. €60.

Sheraton Pine Cliffs Algarve

Pinhal do Concelho ☎289 500 102, ⓦwww.pinecliffs.com. Set in a wooded complex of villas and sports facilities just back from the cliffs between Vilamoura and Olhos de Água – with its own lift down to the beach – this is one of the classiest hotels in the Algarve. Rooms are huge and the best have balconies facing the sea. There are three pools (one indoors), a gym, tennis courts and discounts for the neighbouring golf course, plus disabled access. The grounds include the Porto Pirata, a self-contained children's village where parents can leave their kids in safe hands. €430.

Tivoli Marinotel

Vilamoura marina ☎289 303 303, ⓦwww.tivolihotels.com. This concrete and glass high-rise dominating the south side of the marina has nearly four hundred rooms, most with superb views over the neighbouring beach or marina, and facilities include indoor and outdoor pools, shops and restaurants. €365.

Campsite

Parque do Campiso

Quarteira ☎289 302 821, ⓦorbitur .com, booking for bungalows ☎218 117 070. A well-equipped campsite 1km east of town on the road to Almancil; any bus to or from Faro stops right outside. They also rent out two-tiered wooden bungalows with bathroom and kitchenette sleeping two or four people from €65.

Cafés

Beira Mar

Avda Infante de Sagres 61, Quarteira. Tues–Sun 8am–midnight. Near the tourist office, this bustling *pastelaria* facing the beach makes a superb stop for breakfast or tea, its counter stuffed with delicious homemade cakes and pastries.

Restaurants

O Jacinto

Avda Sá Carneiro, Quarteira ☎289 301 887. Tues–Sun noon–3pm & 7–11pm. Despite its relatively humble appearance, this is one of the best restaurants in the Algarve. There are a few meat dishes, but most people come for superbly cooked fish (from €20) and seafood such as the highly rated Quarteira prawns (around €40 a kilo). Reservations advised.

La Cigale

Olhos de Água ☎289 501 637. Daily 10.30am–midnight. An atmospheric seafood restaurant with an outdoor terrace facing the beach. The fish and seafood are expensive but not outrageously so, and few customers leave disappointed.

Rosa Branca

Marginal, Quarteira ☎289 314 430. Daily 10am–midnight. The best-positioned of a cluster of café-restaurants at the market end of the beach, with fish and grilled meats (from €10) served on outdoor tables facing the sands.

O Tasquinho de Manel

Escola de Vela, Vilamoura ☎289 315 756. Tues–Sun noon–3pm & 7–11pm; lunches only Oct–April. Part of the sailing school on the way to Praia de Falésia, this simple place lacks the pretensions of the marina-side restaurants. Just choose from the moderately priced fish at the counter and enjoy the view from the outdoor tables facing the water.

Bars and clubs

Casino

Vilamoura ☎289 310 000, ⓦsolverde.pt. Daily 4pm–3am. Just south of the marina, Vilamoura's casino hosts a fairly tacky disco (June–Sept nightly 11pm–6am; Oct–May Thurs–Sun 11pm–6am) and lays on regular cabaret-style dance shows and exhibitions.

El Matador

Marina Plaza Loja 66, Vilamoura. Daily noon–1am. With outdoor tables on a cobbled alley and a tiled interior, this has more character (albeit Spanish) than other bars on this stretch. Cocktails and drinks along with a fine range of tapas from around €4.

Kadoc

Estrada de Vilamoura ⓦkadok .pt. June–Sept daily 11.30pm–6am; Oct–May Fri & Sat only 11.30pm–6am. Minimum consumption fee depending on the night. Opposite the Mobil garage on the Vilamoura–Albufeira road, *Kadoc* is the Algarve's biggest club, pulling in up to eight thousand revellers a night, often with international guest DJs.

Sete

Bloco 7, Vilamoura marina ☎289 313 943. Daily 9am–3am. A fashionable chrome-and-steel café-bar part-owned by Portuguese soccer star Luís Figo and named after his shirt number (seven). By day it's a tranquil spot for a coffee or juice, but after dark the sound system cranks up. If you're lucky, one of Figo's mates may pop in – pictures and framed shirts on the wall show previous famous guests.

North of Faro

Though most visitors come to the Algarve for its beaches, it's well worth venturing inland to see some of the variety the region has to offer. Worth a stop is Loulé, famed for its atmospheric Saturday market, while to the north stretches some of the Algarve's least spoilt countryside. Here, the Serra do Caldeirão, dotted with olive and citrus groves, separates the Algarve from the neighbouring region of the Alentejo. Many of its rolling hills are given over to subsistence farming; the fields and orchards are worked as they have been for centuries. This countryside is beautiful terrain for a walk or picnic, especially around Fonte Benémola, Rocha da Pena or the tiny village of Salir with its ruined Moorish castle. Ringed by cork woods, São Brás de Alportel is a sleepy market town with an attractive *pousada* and a quirky museum, while Estói boasts the beautiful gardens of the Palácio de Estói and the fascinating Roman site of Milreu.

Loulé town

Loulé has always been an important market town and its morning market is well worth a visit (see below). It doesn't take long to explore the town's compact centre. The most interesting streets, a grid of cobbled lanes, lie between the remains of its Moorish castle (now a museum) and the thirteenth-century Gothic Igreja Matriz church, with its tall bell tower and palm-lined gardens in front. Some of the streets contain workshops of traditional craftsmen producing leatherwork and copper *cataplanas* (cooking vessels), for sale in many of the local shops.

Loulé market

Loulé's most atmospheric sight is the wonderful covered fruit and vegetable *mercado* (Mon–Sat 8am–3pm), set in a red onion-domed building with Moorish keyhole-style windows. Try and visit on

a Saturday morning, when the market spreads into the surrounding streets – a medley of stalls selling everything from pungent cheeses to cages of live chickens and rabbits. Close by, on Avenida Marçal Pacheco, one block beyond the market, check out the Manueline carvings of coiled ropes on

NORTH OF FARO

0   2 km

▲ FRUIT AND VEGETABLE MARKET, LOULÉ

the façade of the Misericordia church.

Loulé Museu Arqueológico and the castle

Rua D. Paio Peres Correia 17. Tues–Sat 9am–12.30pm & 2.30–5.30pm. €1.10.

The remains of Loulé's castle enclose a small but interesting Museu Arqueológico, housing a range of Roman, Moorish and early Portuguese finds from Loulé and the surrounding area. There are second-century amphorae, ninth-century pots from Salir castle (see p.72) and the foundations of a twelfth-century Moorish house, *in situ* under a glass floor. The largest exhibit is a giant sixteenth-century stone urn, retrieved from the castle itself.

The entry price to the museum allows access to the castle walls, from where you can gaze down over the old town and, on a clear day, see as far as the coast. The entrance is up the steps to the side of the museum, via a kitchen set out in traditional Algarvian style, complete with pots, pans and straw dummies in traditional dress.

Loulé Saturday market and Nossa Senhora da Piedade

Loulé's Saturday-morning gypsy market (from 9.30am) is one of the most colourful in the Algarve. It's around fifteen minutes' walk northwest of the centre – follow the signs to Boliquieme – and takes place on a patch of ground beautifully framed by a pair of dazzling white churches. Stalls sell a motley collection of clothes, ceramics, agricultural produce and general goods, with a separate

▲ VIEW FROM LOULÉ CASTLE WALLS

Visiting Loulé

The bus terminal (☎289 416 655/6) is on Rua Nossa Senhora de Fátima, a couple of minutes' walk north from the old town; there are daily services from Quarteira, Albufeira and Faro. The turismo (May–Sept Tues–Fri 9.30am–7pm, Sat & Mon 9.30am–12.30pm & 2–6pm; Oct–April Tues–Fri 9.30am–5.30pm, Sat & Mon 9.30am–1pm & 2–5.30pm; ☎289 463 900) is on Avenida 25 de Abril, close to the park. A good time to visit Loulé is in July, when it hosts an annual Jazz Festival featuring top international musicians at weekends.

section selling plants and flowers over the road – though much of the colour comes from the market traders themselves.

The market is peered over by the beehive-shaped Nossa Senhora da Piedade – steps wind up to its hilltop position from the far side of the market. At Easter, the church is the starting point of a procession into town for **Mãe Soberana**, one of the Algarve's most important religious festivals (see p.184).

Querença and Fonte Benémola

Ten kilometres northeast of Loulé, Querença is an unexceptional village that comes alive in January for a Smoked Sausage Fair (see p.184). It's also the access point for a bucolic protected nature area known as Fonte Benémola, signed from the turn-off to the village; go 3km down a bumpy road, and you come to a small parking bay and information board just off the road. A gentle 5km round walk starts here and meanders through a tranquil wooded valley cut by the Ribeira da Fonte Menalva and interspersed with a series of bubbling natural springs (*fontes*). The walk takes you down a track to a brook whose verdant

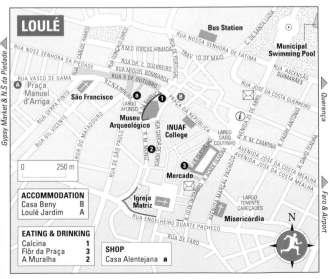

▲ ERMIDA DE PÉ DA CRUZ, SALIN

banks are lined with picnic tables – a popular destination on summer weekends, when a local craftsman often displays basketmaking techniques. At other times you'll share the place only with the resident hoopoes, kingfishers, otters and salamanders, accompanied by a chorus of frogs.

Salir

Set on a hilltop facing rolling countryside, Salir is a beautifully situated agricultural village which retains the vestiges of a Moorish castle. To visit, park by the diminutive Ermida de Pé da Cruz church; from here it's a short stroll along a cobbled track to what's left of the castle – a few low walls and the remains of turrets. The ruins are still being excavated, and though there is little to see, they're in a gorgeous position, the path passing white flower-decked

houses with great views over Salir and the valley beyond.

Rocha da Pena

Rocha da Pena is a craggy limestone hill protecting rare flora and fauna, including mongoose, eagle owls, buzzards and Bonelli's eagles. You'll need to walk to the hill itself for a likely chance to see any of these – there's a waymarked trail across it from near Pena, another totally unspoilt, tiny, agricultural village.

São Brás de Alportel

Though hardly the region's most attractive town, São Brás de Alportel is home to one of the Algarve's more appealing museums. Just east of the main square, on Rua Dr. José Dias Sancho 61, the **Museu Etnográfico do Trajo Algarvio** (☎289 840 100, Ⓦwww.museu-trajo-algarve .web.pt; Mon–Fri 10am–1pm

Visiting São Brás de Alportel

Regular buses from Faro pull into the main square, Largo São Sebastião, a fairly dull space with a couple of banks. There's a small tourist office at no. 23 (May–Sept Mon–Fri 9.30am–12.30pm & 2–6pm; Oct–April Mon–Fri 9.30am–1pm & 2–5.30pm; ☎289 843 165, Ⓔturismo.saobras@rtalgarve.pt;), which supply maps of the town.

& 2–5pm, Sat 7 Sun 2–5pm; €2), housed in an old mansion, has alcoves and corridors full of traditional costumes. At the back, a series of buildings round a courtyard contains cork-cutting equipment, ancient donkey carriages, saddles, bull carts and an old loom. Occasional demonstrations of the machinery take place and, outside in the courtyard, you can walk down steps to the bottom of a traditional well which has been partly excavated.

From the museum, cut down Rua Nova de Fonte and you'll reach the **Jardim da Verbena** (May–Sept 8am–8pm; Oct–April 8am–5pm; free), a wonderful little garden with an open-air swimming pool (hours as park; free). Just west of here lie the narrow streets of the oldest part of town, clustered round the church of Senhor dos Passos (signposted Igreja Matriz), from where there are lovely views of the surrounding valleys.

Palácio do Visconde de Estói

Regular buses from Faro. Estói, a typical inland village, is famous for the delightful peach-coloured Palácio do Visconde de Estói, now a pousada. This is a diminutive version of the Rococo palace of Queluz near Lisbon, built by the Visconde de Carvalha at the end of the eighteenth century. Its verdant *jardim* (garden), reached via a palm-lined avenue near the handsome Igreja Matriz church, is open to the public (Tues–Sat 9am–12.30pm & 2–5.30pm; free). The grounds extend below a terrace dotted with statues of Portuguese literary figures –

Cork

São Brás has traditionally been the Algarve's main centre for cork since it became a major export in the nineteenth century, and nowadays Portugal produces an astonishing fifty percent of the world's cork supplies.

Cork consists of a layer of spongy cells that appear under the bark during the first year of a tree's growth. As the tree grows, the cells grow radially outwards to form a durable, impermeable material with excellent thermal insulation. The cork thus acts as a barrier against pests, extremes of temperature and even fire, allowing the trees to thrive even in barren landscapes. Most importantly, cork is able to regenerate even when a layer is destroyed. Not just once, but throughout the life cycle of a tree, new layers replace those that are cut off, and what's more, the new layers are thicker than the ones they replace. Cork farmers therefore strip away the cork layer without harming the tree, using a curved axe. Around the harvesting time of July and August, you'll see piles of cork bark throughout the region. Trees are harvested every nine years or so, allowing the cork to grow to around 6cm thick – the perfect thickness for wine corks. The white numbers painted on the trees show the year they are next due to be harvested. Most of the trees survive for over a century – one tree in the neighbouring Alentejo district is known to be 220 years old.

Because cork stripping is strictly regulated, the areas where the trees grow tend to be superb protected habitats for wildlife, and few forms of cultivation are as self-sustaining. However, the growing popularity of plastic and screw-top stoppers – and the corresponding avoidance of cork taint – is threatening the livelihood of cork farmers. Already some cork groves are being replaced with more viable crops and there is a danger that an ancient, sustainable environment will be destroyed.

▲ THE GATE TO THE PALÁCIO DO VISCONDE DE ESTÓI

churches in the world. The other recognizable remains are of a bathing complex southwest of the villa, which had underfloor heating, with fragments of fish mosaics; and the apodyterium, or changing room, with its stone benches and arched niches below for clothes. Many of the busts from the site – including those of Hadrian and Empress Agrippina Minor – are on display in Faro's archeological museum (see p.53).

Camões, Herculano and Garrett – along with the Marquês de Pombal, who helped rebuild much of the country after the Great Earthquake of 1755. Look out, too, for some beautiful eighteenth-century *azulejos* of plants and tropical birds.

Milreu

Rua de Faro ☎289 997 823, ⓦwww .ippar.pt. Tues–Sun: April–Sept 9.30am–12.30pm & 2–6pm; Oct– March 9.30am–12.30pm & 2–5pm. €2. The Roman site at Milreu, a ten-minute walk downhill from Estói's main square, is one of the most important Roman sites in Portugal. It predated Faro and was inhabited from the second to the sixth century AD. The site is relatively small and it's easy to find your way around. Archeological excavations are ongoing, but you can clearly make out the remains of a peristyle villa to the north of the site, dominated by the apse of a temple a little to the south, which was converted into a Christian basilica in the third century AD, making it one of the earliest-known Christian

Accommodation

Casa Beny

Rua de São Domingos 13, Loulé ☎289 417 702. A tastefully renovated town house offering plush rooms, with cable TV and bathroom. The roof terrace has great views over the main street – which can be noisy. €60.

Loulé Jardim Hotel

Praça Manuel de Arriaga 23, Loulé ☎289 413 094, ⓦloulejardimhotel .com. Facing a quiet square, this friendly hotel has small but well-decorated en-suite rooms set round an internal courtyard. There's also a bar and a small rooftop pool, while breakfast is a fine buffet spread of fruit, breads and preserves. €75.

Pousada de São Brás

São Brás de Alportel ☎289 845 171, ⓦwww.pousadas.pt. A terracotta-tiled 1940s building set on a hillside 2km north of São Brás de Alportel. The views from the comfortable rooms' balconies are splendid, and there's a pool, tennis courts, games room and expensive restaurant (see opposite). Advance booking is essential in summer; rates tumble in winter. €175.

Cafés

Café Calcina

Praça da República, Loulé. Mon–Fri 8am–11pm, Sat 8am–4pm. A highly atmospheric little café with marble tabletops and black-and-white photos of old Loulé on the walls. The perfect spot for *pastéis de nata* (custard cream tarts), *pastéis de bacalhau* (dried cod rissoles) or a beer with *tremoços* (pickled lupin seeds).

Vanessa

Largo da Liberdade 45, Estói. Mon & Wed–Sun 8am–10pm. The best of the cafés on Estói's main square, with outside tables facing the church. Choose from a good range of tasty sandwiches, toasts and cakes.

Restaurants

Flôr da Praça

Rua José Fernandes Guerreiro 44, Loulé ☎ 289 462 435. Mon–Sat

▲ THE ROMAN SITE OF MILREU

12.30–2.30pm & 7.30–11.30pm. Bargain fish and grills are served in this large, characterful restaurant opposite the market, its walls decorated with old photos, seashells and soccer memorabilia. Full meals for around €14.

Mouro Bar Castelo

Rua Egas Moniz 22, Salir ☎ 289 410 480. Mon & Wed–Sun noon–10pm. This simple café-restaurant near Salir castle serves drinks and Portuguese nosh at decent prices; the dining room commands superb views over the valley.

A Muralha

Rua Martim Moniz 39, Loulé ☎ 289 412 629. Tues–Sat noon–3pm & 7–11pm, Mon 7–11pm. With a flower-filled patio and *azulejo* panels of old Loulé decorating the interior, this is one of the most popular tourist spots in town. Grills are moderately priced (from €12) though unexceptional, while the pricier, more elaborate meat and seafood dishes such as *arroz de marisco* and meat fondues are good bets. There's also a children's menu, and live music on Saturday evenings.

Pousada de São Brás

São Brás de Alportel ☎ 289 845 1712. Daily noon–2.30pm & 7.30–9pm. This *pousada* restaurant commands superb views over the surrounding valleys. International and Portuguese cuisine is well prepared and not too outrageously priced (unlike the wine list), though some may find the service overly formal. Book ahead in summer.

Olhão and around

Earthy and characterful, Olhão's old town is a warren of Moorish-style houses fronted by attractive riverside gardens and a great market. Its harbour is protected by two sandspit islands, Ilha da Culatra and Ilha da Armona, each with superb Atlantic-facing beaches. The latter can also be reached from Fuzeta, a delightful fishing village with its own river beach. The *ilhas* protect a marshy lagoon, part of the Reserva Natural da Ria Formosa, which can be visited from Quinta da Marim, an environmental centre.

Olhão

Beyond its built-up outskirts, Olhão's old town has an immediate charm. The kernel of narrow, pedestrianized streets and flat roofs is reminiscent of North Africa, testimony to the town's centuries-old trading links with Morocco. There are few sights as such. The most prominent building is the unspectacular seventeenth-century parish church of **Nossa Senhora do Rosário** (daily 9am–noon & 3–6pm). Outside, round the back, an iron grille protects the chapel of Nossa Senhora dos Aflitos, where townswomen traditionally gathered to pray for their

OLHÃO & AROUND

▼ FISHERMAN, OLHÃO

menfolk when there was a storm out at sea. Nowadays, curious wax models of children and limbs are placed amid candles as *ex voto* offerings for fertility and cures for ailments. Opposite, at the back of the church of Nossa Senhora da Soledade, lies the small **Museu da Cidade** (Tues–Fri 10am–12.30pm & 2–5.30pm; free), displaying a few archeological finds from the area, from Bronze Age pots to Islamic vases. Upstairs there are relics of the town's industrial heritage, with model fishing boats, oil presses and atmospheric photos.

Visiting Olhão

The train station lies at the northeastern edge of town, off Avenida dos Combatentes da Grande Guerra, some ten to fifteen minutes' walk from the waterfront. The bus terminal (☎289 702 157) is a few minutes away on Rua General Humberto Delgado. The turismo, on Largo Sebastião Martins Mestre (May–Sept Mon–Fri 9.30am–12.30pm & 2–6pm; Oct–April Mon–Fri 9.30am–1pm & 2–5.30pm; ☎289 713 936), can advise on accommodation and give boat times to the *ilhas*. There's also a timetable for ferry services to both islands posted at the ticket kiosk by the quayside; if it's closed you can buy tickets on the ferries.

The other obvious focus of the town is the **market** (Mon–Fri 7am–2pm, Sat 6.30am–3pm), held in the two modern red-brick turreted buildings on the harbourfront. There's meat, fruit and vegetables and cheeses on one side, fish on the other. The fish hall is full of such delights as octopus, scabbard fish and the ubiquitous sardine.

Either side of the market lie shady riverside gardens, complete with kids' play areas and a miniature aviary.

Ilha da Culatra

Ferries from Olhão depart to the Ilha da Culatra throughout the year (June & Sept 6 daily; July & Aug 7 daily; rest of year 4 daily) calling at Culatra (35min, €2.60 return) and Farol (45min, €3.50 return). In summer, an additional service runs between Farol and Faro (see p.55). The Ilha da Culatra is the most populated of the sandspits, its northern, land-facing shore dotted with a series of fishermen's huts between the two main centres at either end of the island, Culatra and Farol. In summer the island's population swells to around three thousand, well supported by a mini market, medical centre and a cluster of seasonal cafés. The easternmost of the settlements is the ferry's first port of call, **Culatra**, the larger of the two, a fairly untidy collection of fishermen's shacks and holiday homes – a boardwalk takes you down to the fine beach. Ten minutes west by boat, **Farol**, the second stop, is far more agreeable. A network of narrow paths links low-rise holiday homes and fishermen's huts clustered round a tall *farol* (lighthouse). Like Culatra, Farol is edged with beautiful tracts of beach on the ocean side, though the mainland-facing beach is grubby. In winter the villages are almost deserted.

If you want to stay on Culatra, ask around at the cafés for private rooms; camping on the island is not encouraged.

▼ THE LIGHTHOUSE AT FAROL

OLHÃO

EATING & DRINKING

A Bote	3
Badial	1
Cais Club	7
Casa Sete Estrelas	5
Gelvi	6
Kinkas	4
Sal e Pimenta	2

ACCOMMODATION

Bela Vista	C
Bicuar	B
Boémia	A

0   100 m

Ilha da Armona

Boats run from Olhão all year round
(June & early Sept 9 departures daily;
July & Aug first departure 7.30am, then
hourly 9am–8pm; late Sept to May 4
daily). 15min; €2 return. With its
miles of attractive, dune-backed
sands, Armona is a very popular
summer destination, though it
doesn't take much of a walk
up the sands to get away from
the crowds. Ferries drop their
passengers at the northern end
of the single settlement on Ilha
da Armona – a long strip of
holiday chalets and huts that
stretches right across the island
on either side of the main
path. Follow the path and it's
a fifteen-minute walk to the
ocean-facing beach. You can
walk along the usually deserted
sands from the Olhão end of

Armona to the eastern end
opposite Fuzeta in about two
hours. For details of Praia da
Fuzeta, see p.80.

There are plenty of bar-
restaurants by the jetty, though
most close out of season, when
it is best to stock up on supplies
from Olhão's market.

Quinta da Marim

Visitor centre daily 9am–12.30pm &
2.30–5.30pm. Park daily: April–Sept
9am–8pm; Oct–March 9am–6pm.
€1.50. Served by regular bus
from Olhão and Fuzeta, Quinta
da Marim is an environmental
educational centre within the
**Parque Natural da Ria
Formosa** in an atmospheric area
of scrubby dunes and mud flats
dotted with pines and gorse. The
reserve is best known for being

the refuge for some unusual poodles that were bred to dive into the water to help chase fish into the fishermen's nets. The poodles were abandoned for more modern methods in the 1950s, though these shaggy canines still thrive here in their purebred form. They can be seen in the park kennels (Mon–Fri 11am–1pm & 2–4pm, Sat & Sun 1–4pm; free; Ⓦ www .caodagau.pt), which feature in a three-kilometre-long nature trail that leads from the car park past various signed highlights: a salt marsh, a freshwater pond where you can sometimes spot rare birds (including, if you're lucky, the rare purple gallinule), a bird recuperation centre and the remains of Roman salting tanks, used for preserving fish. The highlight, at the waterfront, is one of Portugal's last working *moinhos de maré* (tidal mills).

In the middle of the park, a visitor centre has models of traditional fishing boats, fossils, a small aquarium of native fish and a decent café, as well as a roof terrace from where you can admire storks' nests in early summer.

Fuzeta

Fuzeta (or Fuseta) is one of the Algarve's least "discovered" resorts, probably because of its shortage of accommodation. It is not the region's most beautiful town, but it does retain its character as a working fishing village. Indeed, its daily routine revolves round the fishermen, whose colourful boats line the river alongside the town. In summer, the central campsite fills with backpackers, and the two communities usually mingle at the lively café-bars in kiosks that extend in a line from the ferry stop towards the river beach.

The town's straggle of backstreets sits on a low hill facing the lagoon, sheltered by the eastern extremity of Ilha da Armona. Beyond its waterfront of modern shops and apartments lies a river beach, a fine stretch of white sands snaking up to a wooden lifeboat house. In summer many people splash about in the calm waters of the river, though more exhilarating and cleaner waters can be found over the river at Praia da Fuzeta on the Ilha da Armona (see opposite).

Many of the local fish end up at the

▲ QUINTA DA MARIM

Olhão and around **PLACES**

▲ FUZETA WATERFRONT

small covered market on Largo 1° de Maio, the road running parallel to the river; the quayside behind the building is often lined with drying octopus. On Saturdays the market expands into a weekly flea market that lines the adjacent pedestrianized Rua Tenente Barrosa. At other times, everyday goods can be bought from shops around the town's pretty little palm tree-lined central square and Rua da Liberdade, the main shopping Street.

Praia da Fuzeta

Regular ferries (May–Sept roughly every 15min 9am–7pm and often later at busy times; Oct–April 4 daily; check with the ferryman what time the last return leaves; €1.50 return)

Visiting Fuzeta

Fuzeta is on the main Faro–Vila Real train line; the station is ten minutes' walk from the waterfront, at the northern end of Rua da Liberdade. Regular buses from Olhão pull up at the waterfront opposite the campsite.

shuttle from the fishing quay at the back of Fuzeta's campsite to the beach across the lagoon. The narrow Praia da Fuzeta at the eastern end of the Ilha da Armona (see p.78) is one of the finest of the Algarve's sandspit beaches. The beach immediately opposite the ferry stop gets fairly crowded in high summer, but you only have to walk ten minutes or so either way from the holiday beach huts and seasonal drinks kiosks in order to have beautiful, low dune-backed sands all to yourself.

Accommodation

Pensão Bela Vista

Rua Teófilo Braga 65–67, Olhão ☎ & ℱ 289 702 538. An atmospheric little guesthouse, with simple, bright rooms, some completely tiled, arranged around a flower-filled courtyard. Booking advisable. No breakfast. €45.

Pensão Bicuar

Rua Vasco da Gama 5, Olhão ☎ 289 714 816, ⓦ pension-bicuar.net. A characterful Anglo-Danish-run guesthouse on a pedestrianized (but sometimes noisy) central street, with a variety of rooms including family rooms and dorms sleeping up to four. The best are en suite (€10 extra) and have balconies overlooking the old town. There's no breakfast, but you can use the communal kitchen and a superb roof terrace. €35.

Pensão Boémia

Rua da Cerca 20, off Rua 18 de Junho, Olhão ☎ & ℗ 289 714 513. This neat place offers appealing en-suite rooms with TV and a/c, the best with balconies (which cost around €20 extra). It's slightly out of the centre, near the post office, and handy for the bus station. Discounts for longer stays, and breakfast costs extra. €40.

Monte Alegre

Apartadeo 64, Fuzeta ☎ 289 794 222, ℮ monte.alegre@iol.pt. Set in countryside with great coastal views, around 2km northwest of Fuzeta – signed Bias Sul – *Monte Alegre* consists of three well-equipped apartments sleeping up to five, and a superb double room with its own terrace. Run by a friendly German family, there's an outdoor swimming pool, stables for horse rides and a pond full of resident frogs; rooms all have satellite TV and kitchenettes. Minimum stay for some of the year. From €80.

Orbitur Armona

Ilha da Armona ☎ 289 714 173. April–Oct only. The only overnight options on the island are the simple holiday bungalows let out by *Orbitur*, each with their own bathroom. Book ahead in high season. From €56.

Campsites

Parque de Campismo da Fuzeta

Rua da Liberdade, Fuzeta ☎ 289 793 459, ℗ 289 794 034. A beautifully positioned site under trees with its own mini-market, but it gets pretty chock-a-block in high summer.

Parque de Campismo de Olhão

Pinheiros de Marim ☎ 289 700 300, ⓦ www.sbsi.pt/camping. Served by regular bus from Olhão, this upmarket campsite opposite Quinta da Marim is set in substantial grounds with its own pool, kids' playground, tennis courts, mini-market, restaurant and bars; there is even live music some nights.

Cafés

Beira Mar 18

Fuzeta. Mon–Sat 7am–midnight. Opposite the ferry stop, this wooden shack with a few outdoor tables is where the fishermen enjoy their Super Bock beers from dawn onwards. Always lively and usually packed with locals, it also does simple meals and superb *pastéis de bacalhau* (dried cod rissoles).

Café Gelvi

Mercado, Avda 5 de Outubro, Olhão. Tues–Sun 8am–midnight. A bustling *pastelaria*, *geladaria* and *croissanteria* in the corner of the fish market, with outdoor seats facing the water.

Restaurants

Badial

Rua Vasco da Gama 2, Olhão ☎ 289 715 276. Daily 11am–3pm

& 6–10.30pm. A welcoming Indian restaurant in a fine old building, with good-value dishes of the day and some superb fish and prawn curries. Also good for vindaloos (originally a Portuguese dish from Goa), kormas and the like.

A Bote

Avda 5 de Outubro 122, Olhão ☎289 721 183. Mon–Sat 11am–4pm & 7pm–midnight. Always popular, this bustling restaurant, close to the fish market, serves mid-priced fish and meat cooked on a grill and accompanied by mounds of potatoes and salad.

Capri

Praça da República 4, Fuzeta ☎289 793 165. Mon, Tues & Thurs–Sun 10am–midnight. A lively bar-restaurant with tables on the main square. Simple, inexpensive dishes include hit-and-miss fish of the day and more reliable grills and omelettes from €6.

Kinkas

Avda 5 de Outubro 46–48, Olhão ☎289 703 333. Daily 11am–midnight. Opposite Olhão's market, *Kinkas* is known for its fine steaks, though it also does a range of fish and rice dishes and a few veggie options from around €9.

Skandinavia

Rua Tenente Barroso 11, Fuzeta ☎289 793 853. Mon & Wed–Sun 11am–midnight. Near the market, this is the first choice in Fuzeta, with excellent fish and meat from around €8. Specialities include a *cataplana* stew with clams and fish or meat. Tables spill onto a pedestrianized street.

Bars

Cais Club

Mercado, Olhão ☎965 554 732. Daily 10pm–4am. The liveliest of the row of bars behind the market, with outdoor tables facing the water – though most locals hit the inside bar or neighbouring dance area as the music cranks up.

Casa Sete Estrelas

Trav Alexandre Herculano 6, Olhão. Tues–Sun noon–midnight. A highly atmospheric little *tasca* bar serving an inexpensive dish of the day and dirt-cheap wine straight from the barrel. Football-themed decor and oodles of character.

Sal e Pimenta

Rua Alexandre Herculano 48, Olhão ☎289 701 269. Daily noon–midnight. A small, well-run tapas bar with a few outdoor tables. Along with tasty tapas, made with organic ingredients, there are a few light meals such as chicken kebabs, as well as superb chocolate pie.

Tavira and around

Despite its inland position, Tavira is a bustling, if low-key, resort. Set on both sides of the gently flowing Rio Gilão, its highly picturesque old town is a graceful ensemble of church spires and eighteenth-century, crumbling white mansions with hipped terracotta roofs and wrought-iron balconies. There is the inevitable ring of new apartments radiating outwards, but a lively fishing trade along the riverfront injects atmosphere and interest. Most visitors are lured here by the spectacular local sandspit beach, the Ilha de Tavira – the fact that it can only be reached by ferry or by toy train adds to the fun. A more traditional village lies nearby, too: the atmospheric fishing port of Santa Luzia, known as "the capital of the octopus".

The castle

Mon–Fri 8am–5pm, Sat & Sun 9am–5pm. Free. The ruins of Tavira's Castelo lie half hidden amid landscaped gardens. There has been a fort here since Phoenician times, though the current structure dates from the thirteenth century, and parts were rebuilt in the seventeenth century. From the walls there are great views over the town's distinctive curved terracotta rooftops and many churches.

TAVIRA & AROUND

▼ TAVIRA ROOFTOPS

Torre de Tavira

Calçada da Galeria 12. Mon–Sat: April–Sept 9.30am–5.30pm; Oct–March 9am–5pm; tours every 30min. €4. Opposite the castle, you can take a lift to the top of the hundred-metre-high Torre de Tavira, a former water tower that now acts as an interesting Câmara Obscura – with images of the town projected onto a white disc, together with commentary in English.

Santa Maria do Castelo

Of Tavira's 37 churches the large, whitewashed Santa Maria do Castelo is the most impressive. It was built in the thirteenth century and restructured in the eighteenth century in Renaissance style. It contains the tomb of Dom Paio Peres Correia, who reconquered much of the Algarve from the Moors, including Tavira itself in 1242. Fittingly, the church stands on the site of the former mosque. Opposite, the former Convento da Nossa Senhora da Graça is one of the county's top *pousadas* (see p.88).

Palácio Galeria

Calçada da Galeria. Tues–Sat 10am–12.30pm & 2–5.30pm. Admission charge for some exhibitions. The fine Palácio Galeria hosts regular temporary exhibitions of local and international artists, and the sixteenth-century palace itself – with sixteen windows and sixteen roofs – is worth the entrance fee alone.

Igreja da Misericórdia

Tues–Sat 9.30am–12.30pm & 2–6pm. The facade of the Igreja da Misericórdia, just downhill from the Galeria, is a fine example of the Manueline style of architecture. Built between 1541 and 1551 by André Pilarte, the mason who worked on Belém's famous Jeronimos monastery in Lisbon, the church's carved stone doorway depicts a series of mermaids, angels and saints, including Peter and Paul, though the most visible carvings are a couple of lute-playing figures in the doorframe. The striking *azulejo*-lined interior shows scenes from the life of Christ, below an impressive wooden vaulted ceiling.

The south bank

With its tranquil vistas and palm-lined gardens, the south bank of the riverfront is the best part of Tavira for a wander. Here, the former town market building, **Mercado da Riberia**, has become a "cultural centre" – actually a handful of small boutiques and appealing waterfront cafés. The old market walls are also used for temporary exhibitions, usually the works of local artists and photographers.

Past the fish market (for the trade only) fishing boats dock as far as the flyover; appropriately, along this stretch of river lie various slightly pricey and

---

Visiting Tavira

Tavira's bus terminal (☏281 322 546) is by the river, two minutes' walk to the main square, Praça da República, while the train station lies 1km southeast of the square. Up the steps just off Praça da República is the turismo, at Rua da Galeria 9 (May–Sept Tues–Thurs 9.30am–7pm, Fri–Mon 9.30am–12.30pm & 2–6pm; Oct–April Tues–Thurs 9.30am–5.30pm, Fri–Mon 9.30am–1pm & 2–5.30pm; ☏281 322 511, ⊛www.cm-tavira.pt). If you're arriving by car, note there is a complicated one-way system in the central area; it is best to head for the car park under the flyover taking traffic east; follow signs to Quatro Águas (which is reached by heading under the flyover and following the river). A fun way to get your bearings of the town is by taking the toy train, which does a circuit of the old town daily every hour or so (10am–dusk; €4). Sport Nautica, Rua J. Pessoa 26 (☏281 324 943), offers bike rental from €5 a day.

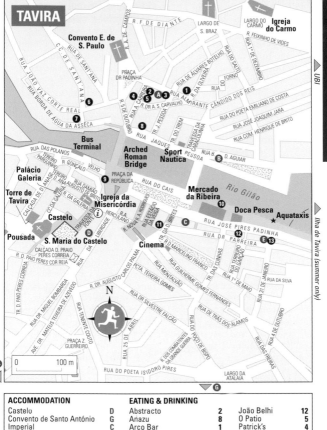

ACCOMMODATION

Castelo	D
Convento de Santo António	G
Imperial	C
Lagôas	A
Marés	E
Princesa do Gilão	B
Quinta do Caracol	F

EATING & DRINKING

Abstracto	2
Anazu	8
Arco Bar	1
Barquinha	13
Beira Rio	7
Bica	3
Cota	6
João Belhi	12
O Patio	5
Patrick's	4
Ribeirinha	10
Tavira Romana	9
Tavirense	11

touristy fish restaurants. Just before the flyover, summer **ferries** depart for the beach and you can also take boat trips (see p.88). Head under the bridge and you'll see the large new town **market** (Mon–Sat 8am–1.30pm) – it's housed in a dull concrete box but has a wonderfully atmospheric and bustling interior, filled with a huge array of fruit and vegetables.

The north bank

Most enjoyably reached over the pedestrianized bridge – built in 1667 on the foundations of a Roman structure – the old streets to the north of the river harbour many of the town's best restaurants. A couple of churches also warrant a visit. Facing the leafy Praça Dr. Padinha is the seventeenth-century **Convento dos Ermistas de São Paulo**, with an unusually large porch.

Five minutes east lies the austere Carmelite church, **Igreja do Carmo**, which holds a famous Christmas concert. You can cross back to the south bank on a low central bridge, put up by the army after floods in 1989 as a temporary structure, and which has held firm ever since.

Ilha de Tavira

Ilha de Tavira is the largest of the Algarve sandspit islands, some 14km in length and backed by nothing but tufted dunes. The beach here is one of the most spectacular in the entire Algarve and also boasts some of the region's warmest waters (over 20°C in summer).

In high summer, the nearest stretch of beach to the ferry terminal is packed with families and a largely Portuguese crowd, though you only have to walk fifteen minutes or so to be clear of the crowds, and out of season you'll probably have the place entirely to yourself.

To get to the beach, head down the path which runs from the jetty through a small chalet settlement, and you'll find beach umbrellas, pedaloes and half a dozen bar-restaurants.

Vila Galé Albacora and the tuna fishing museum

Museum: daily 10am–6pm. Free.

East of the Rio Gilão opposite Quatro Águas, the plush *Vila Galé Albacora* hotel (see p.89) was built in the 1940s as a self-contained fishing village, where tuna fishermen spent the season with their families. The small but informative museum here shows how important tuna was to the area. Until the mid-twentieth century, fleets of forty or so boats set up in formation known as an *armação*, designed to guide tuna into the centre of a system of nets. The best ever catch was in 1881, when 43,000 tuna were netted, but by the 1970s, the annual catch had dwindled to virtually nothing and the industry collapsed. Today, former houses have been turned into hotel rooms, though the village's chapel is still used, and the former school is now a children's club. The route to the hotel passes a series of *salinas*, salt extraction plants which supply fifty percent of Portugal's salt using an evaporation system that has little changed since Roman times.

▼ ILHA DE TAVIRA

▲ THE FERRY TO ILHA DE TAVIRA

Cascatas Moinhos da Rocha

Set in bucolic countryside 7km north of Tavira, the *cascatas* (waterfalls) of Moinhos da Rocha are a popular summer picnic spot for Portuguese families. A series of wooden decks and bridges skirts a leafy ravine sheltering the crystal-clear waters of a small stream. This culminates in a low but nevertheless impressive waterfall that empties into a little lake – it's used as a water source, so you should avoid swimming in it.

Santa Luzia

Billing itself as "King of the Octopus" (the main local catch here), Santa Luzia is an earthy, no-nonsense fishing village famed for its seafood restaurants. You'll see octopus traps lining the small but lively fishing harbour, from where seasonal boat tours run out to the Ilha

de Tavira (see opposite). The village's palm-lined gardens are a delight, and its atmospheric backstreets of tile-fronted houses merit a wander.

Pedras d'El Rei and Praia de Barril

Served by 6 buses daily from Tavira's bus station (Mon–Fri only). *Pedras d'El Rei* is a fairly upmarket holiday complex (see p.89), which offers access to another stretch of the Ilha de Tavira at Barril. From the bus stop and car park next to *Pedras d'El Rei*, cross the causeway to the terminal of a rather ancient-looking **miniature train** (daily

▼ RELICS OF THE TUNA FISHING INDUSTRY, BARRIL

Visiting Ilha de Tavira

Direct ferries (July–Sept daily 8.30am–dusk, roughly hourly; €1.50 return) serve the island from Tavira's riverfront (see p.85). Alternatively, you can take a bus (July to mid-Sept Mon–Fri roughly hourly) from the bus station in Tavira for the ten-minute trip to the jetty at Quatro Águas, or you can walk there in half an hour. From here, ferries (Easter–June 8.30am–7.30pm; July–Sept 8.30am–9pm; Oct–Easter 9am–dusk; €1.30 return) take just five minutes. Note timetables are fairly loosely adhered to and the frequency of the service largely depends on how busy things are: in high season they run every fifteen minutes or so, often until much later than 9pm; at other times they run roughly hourly; always check with the ferryman what time the last boat returns. Another option is aquataxis (daily 8am–5pm, ☎964 515 073), which do the ride for €6 per person from Quatro Águas, €15 from Tavira. The aquataxis also offer one-hour tours of the lagoon for around €10 (minimum of three people).

8.30am–dusk, roughly every 15–30min; €1 single, free to *Pedras d'El Rei* guests). This shuttles across the mud flats – past thousands of fiddler crabs – to the beach of **Barril** on the Ilha de Tavira. You can also walk alongside the tracks in ten to fifteen minutes. At the beach, attractive houses once belonging to fishermen have been turned into a cluster of slightly pricey café-restaurants; there's also a small shop, showers and toilets. After a few minutes' walk right or left of the terminus – past lines of rusting anchors wedged into the dunes – you come to a beautiful, dune-fringed beach stretching for miles.

Accommodation

Pensão do Castelo

Rua da Liberdade 22, Tavira ☎281 320 790, ℻281 320 799. A rambling, very centrally located place, offering enormous clean rooms all with marble floors, TVs and bathrooms; the front rooms can be noisy. Disabled access. €60.

Pousada Convento da Graça

Rua D. Paio Peres Correia, Tavira ☎281 389 040, ⊛www.pousadas.pt. Set in a sixteenth-century former convent around beautiful cloisters and with its own church, this *pousada* is hard to fault. Most of the plush rooms overlook the old town or the pool at the back, nestled within part of the old town walls. During renovation work, the remains of a Moorish settlement were found and these can be viewed through a glass partition in the fashionable bar. There's also a highly rated, if pricey, restaurant that uses local ingredients. €210.

Convento de Santo António

Rua de Santo António, Tavira ☎281 321 573, ℻281 325 632. Closed Jan. With just seven double rooms and a "superior" chapel room, it is best to book ahead (fax only) to bag a place in this elegant sixteenth-century convent with roof terrace. There's also a swimming pool, and breakfast is served in the tranquil courtyard. Minimum stay of four nights in summer; two in winter. €150.

Residencial Imperial

Rua José Pires Padinha 24, Tavira ☎281 322 234, ⊜residencial .imperial@gmail.com. A small *residencial* above a decent restaurant; the nicest rooms overlook the gardens and river. All rooms have TV and shower, though they're on the small side. €60.

Residencial Lagâos

Rua Almirante Cândido dos Reis 24, Tavira ☎ 281 322 252. A characterful place on the north side of the river with small, simple en-suite rooms clustered round an upstairs patio. There's also a communal roof terrace. The price does not include breakfast. €50.

Residencial Marés

Rua José Pires Padinha 134–140, Tavira ☎ 281 325 815, ⓦ residencialares.com. Twenty-four spotless rooms, some on the small side but all with a/c, TV, *azulejos* and some with balconies over the river or old town. There's a great roof terrace and a communal sauna, too. €80.

Pedras d'el Rei

☎ 281 380 600, ⓦ www.pedrasdelrei .com. Perfect for families, this well-established holiday village consists of a series of spacious apartments and villas set in beautifully landscaped grounds. There's a central lawned area focused on an outdoor pool and overlooked by a café, bar and a restaurant. Facilities include a playground, children's club and well-stocked shop; there's also an aviary, and residents have free passes for the train to the beach. Apartments from €100.

Residencial Princesa do Gilão

Rua Borda d'Água de Aguiar 10–12, Tavira ☎ 281 325 171, ⓔ residencial

-gilao@hotmail.com. This friendly *residencial* stands right on the quayside, a modern, white building with *azulejo*-decorated interior. Rooms are tiny but have their own shower rooms and small balconies (those at the front overlook the river). €50.

Quinta do Caracol

Tavira ☎ 281 322 475, ⓦ quintacaracol .pa.net.pt. Set in lawned grounds north of the train station, this lovely farmhouse offers self-catering apartments sleeping two to five people in tastefully converted outbuildings. There are tennis courts, a tiny plunge pool, children's play area and bikes for rent. €120.

Vila Galé Albacora

☎ 281 380 800, ⓦ www.vilagale .pt. A fascinating former tuna-fishing village (see p.86) has been tastefully converted into a four-star hotel. The best rooms face the river estuary; others face a car park or the enormous, flower-filled central courtyard. This also has a large pool, games room, restaurant and bar; inside there's another pool and health club. Courtesy public transport serves Tavira and the beach. The downside of its riverside position is a colony of voracious mosquitoes. €175, or €210 for river views.

▼ THE ROMAN BRIDGE, TAVIRA

Campsite

Camping Ilha de Tavira

℡281 321 709, ⓦwww.campingtavira
.com. Easter–Sept. Set under trees a
minute from the sands and with
a well-stocked mini-market,
this campsite draws a youthful
crowd. There's a kids' play area
and ATM, too, though the site
gets packed in July and August.

Cafés

Anazu

Rua Jacques Pessoa 11–13, Tavira.
Daily 8am–midnight. A lovely, tile-
fronted riverfront café which
catches the sun all day – a good
place for breakfast or a sunset
drink. There's a games room/
cybercafé attached.

Ribeirinha

Mercado da Ribeira, Loja 3, Tavira.
Daily 9am–9pm, closed Thurs Oct–May.
One of the best positioned of
the old market café-restaurants,
this is a fine spot for a beer or
simple meal overlooking the
river. Does good *bitoque* (steak
sandwiches) and salads.

Tavira Romana

Praça da República 24–26, Tavira.
Daily 8am–midnight. You can get
great cakes and a huge variety
of home-made ice creams at
this café with outdoor seats on
a pedestrianized stretch, a fine
place for people-watching.

Restaurants

Abstracto

Rua António Cabrita 34, Tavira
℡917 043 274. Wed–Sun 7–11pm.
A great place, with jazzy decor,
for innovative international
dishes such as salmon with

tomatoes and clams, prawn
curry or garlic duck. Mains
from around €13.

Barquinha

Rua José Pires Padinha 142, Tavira
℡281 322 843. Mon, Tues &
Thurs–Sun noon–3pm & 7–10pm.
Squeezed between a row of
somewhat touristy restaurants,
this place remains refreshingly
low-key and moderately priced.
You can get excellent *bacalhau
à brás* and other grills, best
washed down with the house
wine at the outside tables as
you watch the swifts wheeling
over the river.

Beira Rio

Rua Borda d'Água de Assêca 46–50,
Tavira ℡281 323 165. Daily 5–11pm.
A roomy riverside restaurant set
in a former girls' school, with
appealing tree-shaded tables
outdoors. Moderately priced
international dishes include
pasta, salads and vegetarian
dishes; the inside bar area,
complete with fishing boats for
seats, is also worth sampling. Full
meals around €18.

Bica

Rua Almirante Cândido dos Reis 22–24,
Tavira ℡281 323 843. Daily noon–3pm
& 7–10pm. Always busy – book
or get there early to guarantee
a table – this unglamorous
but excellent-value restaurant
serves meat, fish, *cataplanas* and
omelettes from around €7.

Capelo

Avda Eng. Duarte Pacheco, Santa
Luzia ℡281 381 670. Mon–Tues &
Thurs–Sun noon–2am. The top
place to eat in Santa Luzia,
with a spacious, *azulejo*-lined
interior and an outdoor terrace.
There's a lengthy menu of
well-prepared fish and seafood.
Mains from €13.

▲ RESTAURANTE BEIRA RIO

Casa do Abade

Largo da Igreja 5, Santa Luzia
☎281 381 734. Mon–Wed &
Fri–Sun 12.30–2.30pm & 6–9.30pm.
Opposite Santa Luzia's modern
church, *Casa do Abade* is a tiny
place that offers much. It has
a rustic, cosy interior and a
few outdoor tables and serves
superb fish and grills – try
the *arroz de polvo come feijoa*
(octopus rice with beans).
Mains around €15. There is
also a children's menu.

Cota

Rua J.V. Corte Real 38, Tavira ☎281
324 873. Daily noon–3pm & 7.30–
11pm. A good-value *churrasqueira*
serving grilled fish and meats
from around €7. From May to
September meals are served on
the rooftop terrace affording
fine views over town.

João Belhi

Rua José Pires Padinha 96, Tavira
☎965 449 557. Mon & Wed–Sun
noon–3pm & 6.30–10pm. Less
expensive and with more of
a local feel than most of the
restaurants on this stretch, this
place offers a menu featuring
the usual fish and meat dishes
and good house wine. The fried
mixed fish is always delicious.

Pavilhão da Ilha

Ilha de Tavira ☎281 324 131.
March–Oct daily noon–10pm. The
best place on the island for a
full meal, with tasty, moderately
priced fish and grills and a lively
bar area; it's just past the campsite
as you head to the beach.

Quatro Águas

Quatro Águas ☎281 325 329.
Tues–Sun noon–3pm & 7–10pm.
A famous seafood restaurant
specializing in dishes such as
açorda and *cataplana de marisco*
(seafood stews) and *bife de frango
com molho roquefort* (chicken with
Roquefort sauce). Expect to pay
over €20 a head.

Bars and clubs

Patrick's

Rua Dr. António Cabreira 25–27, Tavira
☎281 325 998. Tues–Sat 6pm–1am.
Closed Nov. A welcoming *adega*-
style, English-run bar-restaurant,
where, along with some familiar
beers, you can enjoy bar food
such as piri-piri prawns and
curries.

Santa Loucara

Mercado Municipal Loja 3, Tavira
☎965 412 767. Tues–Sun 10pm–4am.
One of the best of the music
bars along the front of the
market building, with a flat-
screen TV and a lively crowd.

UBI

Rua Almirante Cândido dos Reis, Tavira
☎281 324 577, ⦿www.ubisdisco
.web.pt. July–Sept Tues–Sun
midnight–6am; Oct–June Fri & Sat
only. On the eastern outskirts
of town, Tavira's only disco
is housed in a huge, metallic
warehouse; the locals warm up
with a few pre-clubbing drinks
in the *Bubi Bar* in the same
building (open from 10pm).

The eastern Algarve

Though long popular with Spanish day-trippers, the eastern Algarve is only just being more widely discovered as an alternative destination to the heavily developed central stretch. The pick of the resorts along this part of the coast is the old fishing village of Cabanas, owing to its excellent sandspit beach, the Praia de Cabanas. This spit can also be reached from Fábrica further east, near one of the prettiest villages in the Algarve, Cacela Velha. Beyond here, the sandspit begins to merge with the shoreline to give more accessible beaches at Manta Rota, Altura and Monte Gordo, the eastern Algarve's biggest resort and the last beach stop before the border with Spain.

Cabanas

Cabanas takes its name from the fishermen's "huts" that once lined its palm-fringed riverside. There is still a kernel of atmospheric backstreets made up of colourful fishermen's houses, though these days Cabanas consists largely of low-rise shops, cafés and bars facing a marshy river estuary. Moored boats testify to the continued fishing industry, though the economy is largely driven by tourism thanks to the glorious sands of **Praia de Cabanas**, over the estuary, and the ruins of an old sea fort

crumbling on the shoreline just east of town. Ferries shuttle passengers to the beach from a small jetty at the eastern edge of town (every 15min or so April–Oct 9am–dusk, €1 return). Cross the dunes, and before you stretch miles of golden sand, with a couple of seasonal beach cafés.

Cacela Velha

Perched on a low cliff facing the estuary, the whitewashed village of Cacela Velha is a reminder of how the Algarve must have looked half a century ago. Apart from a couple of simple

▼ CABANAS

café–restaurants, there are no tourist facilities, just a pretty church and the remains of an eighteenth-century fort, and even that is a customs police station and closed to the public. Surrounded by olive groves, and offering exhilarating views from its clifftop, the village is highly picturesque, and despite the golf courses just to the west it's rarely overrun by visitors. Its busiest time is during the four-day Moorish Nights festival in July when a souk is set up along with Arabic food stalls and music.

To reach Cacela Velha by public transport, you need to get the Tavira–Vila Real bus to set you down on the highway, just before Vila Nova de Cacela, from where it's a fifteen-minute walk down a signposted side-road to the village.

The beach below the village, a continuation of **Praia de Cabanas**, is a beautiful, uncrowded long strand of soft sand backed by low dunes. To get to it by car, follow signs to Fábrica, just west of the village, around 1km downhill. There is a good restaurant next to the ferry (daily in summer, but only during good weather the rest of the year; €1 return).

Manta Rota

Regular bus from Vila Real or Monte Gordo. Manta Rota is the first place east of Tavira where the beach is accessible by land. It's a superb, wide stretch of beach backed by a palm-lined square, although the village itself is a characterless splodge of villas and modern apartments. From Manta Rota you can walk along the beach all the way to the eastern edge of Portugal: from Manta Rota it's around thirty minutes to Alagoas, another twenty minutes to Praia Verde, and forty more on to Monte Gordo.

Altura

Further east, Altura is a large, modern and bustling resort spreading inland from another fine beach, Praia de Alagoas. Reached by a boardwalk, the enormous sandy beach is well stocked with beach umbrellas,

▼ THE FORT AT CACELA VELHA

▲ THE BEACH AT MANTA ROTA

bars and watersports facilities, and though the town lacks much character, it's popular with Spanish and Portuguese holiday-makers which gives it a lively feel.

Praia Verde

Regular buses to Vila Real pass the sideroad to Praia Verde. Four kilometres along the main road from Altura, a wide expanse of wooded slopes gives the name to the sands of **Praia Verde** (green beach). Despite the densely packed low-rise blocks that make up the holiday complex hidden in the trees, this remains the least-developed beach along this stretch, with just a couple of seasonal beach cafés and one restaurant. Further east, towards Monte Gordo, the beach becomes more unkempt, backed by scrubby dunes, but the sands are much less likely to be crowded in summer.

Monte Gordo

Monte Gordo ("fat mountain") is the last resort before the Spanish border and the most built-up of the eastern holiday towns. It's unashamedly high-rise, with new buildings going up all the time. In June, expect to see crowds of Harley-Davidson riders who descend for an annual biker's meet; at other times, the plethora of Spanish day-trippers and big spenders lured by the seafront casino (Ⓦwww.solverde.pt) gives the resort a buzz, while the beach, faced by a partly pedestrianized promenade, is wonderfully broad. A fleet of tractors keeps the sands clean at the end of each day, and there are a few colourful fishing boats clustered round the western edge of town.

Walkers can head east up the beach to the mouth of the Rio Guadiana, from where you can stand at the southwesternmost point of Portugal and gaze over the border into Spain – about an hour's walk, past cocklers who dredge the soft sands at low tide.

▲ PRAIA VERDE

Visiting Monte Gordo

Buses from Vila Real and Tavira pull up close to the main Avenida Vasco da Gama at the seafront and adjacent to the casino. At the latter, there are plenty of car parking spaces. Just east of the casino is the turismo (daily: May–Sept 9.30am–7pm; Oct–April 9.30am–5.30pm; ☎281 544 495), which hands out town maps and can give details of private rooms.

Accommodation

Cantinho da Ria Formosa

Ribeira de Junco, Cacela Velha ☎281 951 837, ⊛www.cantinhoriaformosa .com. Around 1km from the beach and the golf course, this whitewashed *residencial* sits in rural solitude on the road to Cacela Velha. Rooms are clean and modern, with views over the garden or fields. There are stables attached, and horse rides are on offer at around €20 an hour. €75.

Eurotel Altura

Altura ☎281 956 450, ⊛www .eurotel-altura.com. A towering three-star hotel dominating the beachfront and offering 135 large rooms, with disabled access, bath, TV and minibar; views from the top-floor rooms are stunning, and there's also an indoor and outdoor pool, games room and tennis courts. €150.

Pedras da Rainha

Cabanas ☎281 380 680, ⊛www .pedrasrainha.com. A well-run little resort with apartments and villas (sleeping up to ten) clustered around pleasant lawns, tennis courts and a large pool, all with disabled access. Two-bed apartments from €100.

Hotel Vasco da Gama

Avda Infante Dom Henrique, Monte Gordo ☎281 510 900, ⊛www .vascodagamahotel.com. If you want to stay on the beach, then this decent high-rise is your best bet. Its slightly old-fashioned ambience gives it some character, and the best rooms have balconies. There are also tennis courts, kids' play areas, a bar and restaurant. All rooms have TVs and en-suite bathrooms. €120, rooms with sea-facing balconies €180.

Campsite

Parque de Campismo Municipal de Monte Gordo

Monte Gordo ☎281 510 970, ⊛www .cm-vrsa.pt. This huge campsite is set under pines out on the Vila Real road, a short walk from the beach where there are plenty of inexpensive restaurants. The facilities are minimal, but the atmosphere is friendly and welcoming.

▲ DOORWAY, MONTE GORDO

Cafés

Casa Azul

Cacela Velha. Mon & Wed–Thurs noon–8pm, Fri & Sat 11am–1pm. By the car park at the entrance to town, this arty space serves as a café, restaurant and small crafts shop – hence a range of tempting gifts, snacks, cakes and caipirinha cocktails.

Jaime

Monte Gordo. Daily 9am–7pm. A simple beach café–restaurant facing the jumble of fishing boats west of the casino, a great spot for a light lunch or sunset beer.

Restaurants

O Costa

Fábrica, Cacela Velha ☎281 951 467. Daily noon–3pm & 7–11pm. Moderately priced fish and grilled meats are served in an idyllic position on a broad terrace facing the waters.

Das Mares

Praia de Alagoas, Altura ☎281 956 563. May–Sept Mon & Wed–Sun 10am–3pm & 7–10pm; Oct–April Mon & Wed–Sun 10am–3pm. The best of Altura's seafront café-restaurants, serving fine seafood, salads and omelettes right on the sands, at prices that won't burn a hole in your wallet (mains around €9).

Finalmente

Manta Rota ☎281 952 980. Mon & Wed–Sun noon–11pm. On the road into Manta Rota, this is a highly characterful place with walls decked in agricultural implements and curios. The outside terrace has shell-encrusted tables under an ivy-covered canopy. Food is equally inviting, with a long list of *bacalhau* dishes from €10,

plus more pricey rice dishes and paella.

O Firmo

Monte Gordo ☎281 513 280. Daily noon–10pm. On the beach in front of the casino, this laid-back restaurant offers tasty grills and salads. It's not cheap, but the view from the front terrace can't be faulted, while the back, ivy-clad patio is also appealing. Mains from €10.

A Grelha

Rua José Correia do Nascimento, Cabanas ☎963 452 413. Daily 9am–3pm & 6–11pm. This traditional *tasca* has been given a bright, arty makeover, complete with contemporary paintings of local life on the walls. It does very good dishes, from simple breakfasts to tasty grills (from €9). A little outdoor patio completes its attractions.

Pedro

Rua Capitão Batista Marçal 51, Cabanas ☎281 370 425. Tues–Sun 12.30–3pm & 7–10pm. This attractive restaurant has a terrace facing the estuary. Grills are inexpensive, or pay a little more for the speciality *cataplanas* – including a delicious *cataplana de amêijoas* (with clams) – and tiger prawns.

Pezinhos

Praia Verde ☎281 513 195. Feb–Nov daily 10am–2am. A highly rated beachside restaurant serving expensive fish and seafood in a superb position right on the unspoilt sands.

A Roda

Avda 28 de Maio, Cabanas ☎281 370 239. Daily 12.30–3pm & 7–10pm. An attractive place with a breezy terrace where you can enjoy mid-priced omelettes, salads and fresh fish.

Vila Real, the Guadiana and the Serra de Alcaria

The broad Rio Guadiana forms the Algarve's eastern boundary with Spain. Overlooking the river, the border town of Vila Real is one of the region's most architecturally interesting towns and offers easy access across the border, either by road or a picturesque ferry route.

North of Vila Real, Castro Marim's historical role as a frontier town is still evident in its two spectacular forts, while further border fortifications are evident at the picturesque town of Alcoutim, 40km to the north.

The minor road hugging the river valley in between these two towns is a delight, while travelling inland from Alcoutim you can enjoy the spectacular mountain scenery of the wild Serra de Alcaria, where virtually the only form of tourist development is near Vaqueiros – a mining village theme park, A Cova dos Mouros.

Vila Real

The border town and harbour of Vila Real de Santo António has long been a favoured destination for Spanish day-trippers, lured by Portuguese food and cheap shopping. The original settlement was demolished by a tidal wave at the beginning of the seventeenth century, and the site stood empty until it was revived in 1774 by the Marquês de Pombal, the king's right-hand man. Eager to apply the latest concepts of town planning, Pombal used the same techniques he had already pioneered in Lisbon and rebuilt Vila Real on a grid plan.

The grid focuses on the handsome central square, Praça Marquês de Pombal,

▼ THE MAIN SQUARE, VILA REAL

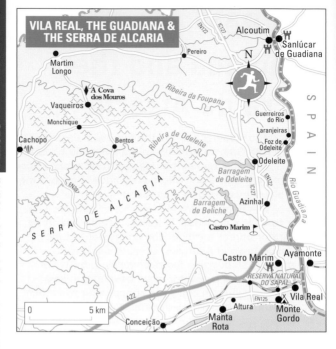

ringed by orange trees and low, white buildings, a couple of which house pleasant outdoor cafés.

Just north of the square, the **Centro Cultural António Aleixo** (Mon–Fri 10am–1pm & 3–7pm; free) on Rua Teófilo Braga, the old market building, has been reborn as an innovative space for temporary exhibits and occasionally films. At Christmas, don't miss the giant Nativity scene erected here, consisting of some 2500 figures.

The surrounding streets have a certain low-key charm, with rows of linen shops, electrical retailers and grocers. The riverside gardens are also attractive, sporting several cafés and affording fine views across the marina to Ayamonte in Spain.

Into Spain: Ayamonte

A fun half-day's excursion is to take the ferry from Vila Real across the Guadiana to Ayamonte in Spain (every 40min from 9am, last return 7pm, which is 8pm Spanish time; €1.40 single). The crossing takes twenty minutes,

Visiting Vila Real

Vila Real is the eastern terminal of the Algarve railway, and the station lies five minutes' walk north of the waterfront; turn left out of the station to get there. Buses (℡281 511 807) stop right on the riverfront itself or at the terminus just north of the train station. The turismo (Mon–Fri 10am–1pm & 3–7pm; ℡281 542 100) is situated in a corner of the old market building on Rua Teófilo Braga.

VILA REAL DE SANTO ANTONIO

RUA DE AYAMONTE

Bus Station

N

RUA DR. MANUEL ARRIAGA

RUA JOSE BARAO

AVENIDA DA REPÚBLICA

Rio Guadiana

RUA DR. SOUSA MARTINS

RUA A. CAPA

RUA C.F. RAMIREZ

RUA DA PRINCESA

Marina

RUA CANDIDO DOS REIS

A ❶

RUA TEÓFILO BRAGA

B

❷ *i* ❸

RUA DOM PEDRO V

❹

PR. MARQUES DE POMBAL

Centro Cultural António Aleixo

RUA 5 DE OUTUBRO

RUA 1 DE MAIO

RUA GENERAL HUMBERTO DELGADO

RUA DO BRAZIL

0   50 m

R. C. DA GRANDE GUERRA

❺

Monte Gordo & EN125 ▽

ACCOMMODATION	
Baixa Mar	B
Guadiana	A

EATING & DRINKING	
Os Arcos	5
Arelinha	4
Cantinho de Marquês	3
Caves do Guadiana	1
O Coração da Cidade	2

PLACES   Vila Real, the Guadiana and the Serra de Alcaria

and is a fine ride, with the forts of Castro Marim visible to the west and the impressive bridge to the north.

Ferries stop at Ayamonte's dull waterfront, but when you head 200m or so inland to Plaza de la Laguna you'll quickly realize you are in Spain: it's a delightful palm-lined square with bright, Moorish-influenced tiled benches. Just south of the square is the town's handsome church, Parroquia de las Angustias, around which is a warren of characterful backstreets, the shops seeming spruce and upmarket in comparison with Vila Real's.

South of the church is another square, the long, palm-fringed Plaza de la Ribeira, adjacent to some small docks and surrounded by inexpensive cafés and tapas bars.

Castro Marim and around

The village of Castro Marim was once a key fortification protecting Portugal's southern

coast. Nowadays it's a sleepy place that only really comes alive in late August when it holds the **Medieval Days festival**, with jousting, lute players and craft stalls. The festival commemorates the fact that Castro Marim was the first headquarters for the Order of Christ, who were based at a huge **castle** (daily: April–Oct 9am–7pm; Nov–March 9am–5pm; free), built by Afonso III in the thirteenth century and rebuilt during the War of Restoration in 1640. The little chapel inside the castle was regularly visited

▲ THIS WAY TO SPAIN, VILA REAL

Visiting Castro Marim

Buses to Castro Marim from Vila Real (several daily Mon–Fri, 2–3 at weekends) pull up near the tourist office on the main Rua de São Sebastião. The turismo is on Rua José Alves Moreira 2–4, next to a tiny square, Praça 1º de Maio (Mon–Fri 9.30am–1pm & 2–5.30pm; ☏281 531 232), just below the castle, with an attractive café.

by Henry the Navigator. Most of the castle was destroyed in the Great Earthquake of 1755, with only the gate and outer walls surviving, though ongoing excavations show even earlier remains going back to Roman and Iron Age times. You can clamber up the walls for fine views across the mud flats of the Reserva Natural do Sapal and the impressive modern suspension bridge to Spain.

Further fine views are to be had from the smaller thirteenth-century Fortaleza de São Sebastião, whose recently renovated ruins cap the hilltop opposite.

Reserva Natural do Sapal

The Reserva Natural do Sapal is a wide, flat area of marshland that extends around Castro Marim and is a refuge for some important and unusual wildlife. The turismo in Castro Marim can supply maps with walking routes through the reserve and direct you to the remote reserve headquarters (Mon–Fri 9am–12.30pm & 2–5.30pm; ☏281 510 680). One of the area's most unusual and elusive inhabitants is the extraordinary, ten-centimetre-long, swivel-eyed, Mediterranean chameleon. Though common in North Africa, in Europe it is only found here and in isolated spots in Spain and Crete.

Odeleite and Foz de Odeleite

North of Castro Marim, beyond the IP1 to Spain and the golf course, the fast EN127 heads into the least-visited part of the Algarve. There are some good picnic spots at a couple of attractive **reservoirs** (*barragens*) signposted off the road at Beliche and Odeleite, but the most scenic route is along the sideroad signed to Foz de Odeleite and Alcoutim. Infrequent buses from Vila Real follow the EN122 on school days only, calling at the tiny village of Foz de Odeleite and at Alcoutim.

Foz de Odeleite is an attractive village at the mouth (*foz*) of the Rio Odeleite, a tributary of the Guadiana. Boat trips often stop off here while groups are taken round to see the communal bread ovens and traditional flat roofs of the village, used to dry pumpkins and fruits during the summer months. There are four good marked walks either side of the village; the best is an eleven-kilometre/two-hour return

▲ CASTRO MARIM

trip to the village of Odeleite, signposted along the Rio Odeleite. Alternatively, it's around 15km from Foz de Odeleite to Alcoutim along the Guadiana, a river which Nobel prize-winner José Saramago says "was born beautiful and will end its days beautiful: such is its destiny".

▲ THE RIVER GUADIANA

Gueirreiros do Rio and along the Guadiana

Gueirreiros do Rio is a small, traditional village on the banks of the wide Guadiana, its fertile shores planted with vineyards, citrus groves and almond trees which blossom spectacularly in spring. It's worth a brief stopover for its tiny **Museu do Rio** (Tues–Sun 9am–1pm & 2–5pm; €2.50, ticket valid in the region's Núcleos Museológicos, see p.102). Set in a primary school, the museum consists of sketches, maps, photos and factsheets and a video related to the river's wildlife and history; all the labels are in Portuguese.

Alcoutim

The picturesque village of Alcoutim has a long history as a river port, dominated in turn by Greeks, Romans and Moors who, over the centuries, fortified its riverside hilltop with various structures to protect the copper transported down river from the nearby mines at São Domingos. Nowadays Alcoutim survives largely on tourism, its chief attractions being its tranquil riverside position and the fourteenth-century hilltop **castle** (daily 9am–1pm & 2–5pm; €2.50), a leafy ruin filled with trees and offering fine views over the town and into Spain. The entrance fee includes access to a small **archeological museum** by the main gates, which traces the history of the castle, its active service in the War of Restoration and the Liberal Wars, and the remnants of earlier structures on the site. The same ticket gives access to a rather dull sacred art collection in the nearby Ermida de Nossa Senhora de Conceição, together with other museums in the region (see p.102).

Guadiana boat trips

Various companies offer day cruises up the Guadiana, departing from Vila Real harbour. Some go as far as Alcoutim (see above), around 40km away, others to Foz de Odeleite, around half that distance. Either trip is idyllic, passing through unspoilt, rolling countryside dotted with olive groves, with the opportunity for swimming stops. Prices start at around €50 per person, which includes lunch. Riosul (☏ 281 510 200, ⊛ www.riosultravel.com) and Peninsular (☏ 968 20180, ⊛ www.peninsular.cjb.net) are a good first port of call.

Visiting Alcoutim

Two to three daily buses (Mon–Fri only) from Vila Real pull in adjacent to the small main square, Praça da República, near the turismo (daily: May–Sept Tues–Thurs 9.30am–7pm, Fri–Mon 9.30am–12.30pm & 2–6pm; Oct–April Tues–Thurs 9.30am–5.30pm, Fri–Mon 9.30am–1pm & 2–5.30pm; ☎281 546 179).

From the castle, cobbled backstreets lead down to the small main square, below which lies the appealing riverfront. The river currents are too strong for safe swimming, but off the Mértola road on the edge of town is a small river beach (*praia fluvial*). A few huts front a little bathing area on the banks of the Rio Cadavais – a popular summer spot for picnics.

Into Spain: Sanlúcar

From Alcoutim waterfront, a **ferry** (daily 9am–1pm & 2pm–dusk; €1 single) heads over the Guadiana to the Spanish village of **Sanlúcar**, a mirror image of Alcoutim, with its own ruined castle and lovely views back over Portugal. Although euros are the shared currency, the clocks are still an hour apart, usually chiming slightly out of sync. There's a little café right by the ferry terminal on the other side if you fancy a *café con leche*.

▼ THE RIVER GUADIANA AT ALCOUTIM

Núcleos Museológicos

The Núcleos Museológicos is a collective of small museums set up in otherwise neglected agricultural villages in an attempt to lure visitors out of their cars into the remote but beautiful region around Alcoutim. It's a worthy concept, though none of the museums warrants more than a ten-minute leg stretch. A ticket for €2.50 allows entry to any of the participating museums, valid for a week. Apart from the castle and museum in Alcoutim (see opposite) and Gueirreiros do Rio (see p.101), the museums open on a rotation basis, though at present, those in Pereiro, Giões and Santa Justa are closed. Check with the turismo in Alcoutim for the latest times, or call ☎281 540 509.

At the otherwise unremarkable village of **Martim Longo**, a history museum displays an eclectic collection of maps, agricultural implements, lamps, rugs and old radios. At **Vaqueiros,** a more alluring agricultural museum is dedicated to man's relationship with nature and family life in a rural village; exhibits include olive presses, old measures, pots and pans.

A Cova dos Mouros

☎281 498 505, ⓦwww .minacovamouros.sitepac.pt. Phone for visits by appointment only, €6.50. A Cova dos Mouros is an innovative, German-run theme park built on the site of an ancient gold and copper mine. Discovered in 1865, the mines date back to around 2500

BC. Stone moulds, primitive furnaces for smelting ore, copper axes, chisels and saws, rock tombs and two Roman villas have all been discovered at the site. Subsequently abandoned, the site was bought up in the 1990s and today consists of a replica furnace, reconstructed thatched medieval houses typical of the Serra do Caldeirão, and slightly eery dummies posing as Stone Age figures. The site can be visited in groups of over fifteen people only, but if you phone ahead you can tag onto other group visits. The attractions are linked by a one-kilometre trail which passes old mine shafts and wells. There is also a café and you can walk down to natural pools and take a dip in the Rio Foupana.

The site also acts as a reserve for native wildlife; if you're lucky you might spot deer and rare griffin vultures, and there is also a bird recovery centre.

Accommodation

Baixa Mar
Rua Dr. Teófilo Braga 3, Vila Real ☎281 543 511. A simple guesthouse with small, functional rooms, the best ones at the front with great views over the river towards Spain. It doesn't do breakfast, but there are plenty of cafés nearby on this pedestrianized street. €40.

Estalagem do Guadiana
Alcoutim ☎281 540 120, ⓦwww .grupofbarata.com. Much the smartest place in Alcoutim – head north out of Alcoutim and follow the signs. A swish, modern inn with its own pool, tennis court, restaurant (daily noon–3pm & 7–10pm) and Saturday-night entertainment.

Spacious rooms come with satellite TV, baths and fine river views. €85.

Hotel Guadiana
Avda da República 94–96, Vila Real ☎281 511 482, ⓦwww.hotelguadiana .com.pt. A national monument, with a grand exterior and lavish Art Deco touches, including a fine dining room. The characterful high-ceilinged rooms come with TVs and en-suite bathroom; the best face the river. €70.

Ilda Afonso
Rua Dr. João Dias 10, Alcoutim ☎281 546 211. Just uphill from the main square, this small but spruce, simple *pensão* offers pleasant rooms with their own baths, though the price does not include breakfast. €35.

River Hotel
Guerreiros do Rio ☎281 540 170, ⓦwww.guerreirosdorio.com A smart, contemporary hotel on a bluff just above the village, with its own swimming pool. Plush rooms have great views over the river, as does the in-house restaurant, which serves local specialities such as grilled eels and river fish. The hotel can also detail local walks and arrange trips on the water. €100.

Youth hostel
Alcoutim ☎ & ⓕ281 546 004, ⓦwww .pousadasjuventude.pt. This very smart seventy-bed youth hostel is around 1.5km north of the village, across the Ribeira Cadavais; cross the bridge beyond Praça da República and follow the signs. It has its own pool, canteen, bar and launderette as well as disabled access, and can help with canoe and bike rental. Double rooms from €40; four-bed dorms from €16.

Cafés and bars

Cantinho de Marquês

Praça Marquês de Pombal 24, Vila Real. Mon–Sat 8am–11pm (closes 8pm Oct–April). A busy café with tables spilling out onto the main square under fragrant orange trees. It's the perfect drink stop, and also does mean *pastéis de bacalhau*.

O Coração da Cidade

Rua Dr. Teófilo Braga, Vila Real ☎281 543 303. Daily 8am–11pm. On the corner of Rua Almirante Cândido dos Reis, just north of the market building, this all-purpose café-restaurant sells everything from snacks, drinks and ice creams to full meals. It's always lively downstairs, with tables on the street.

Passage Café

Plaza de la Laguna 11, Ayamonte. Mon–Sat 8am–4.30pm, Sun noon–4.30pm. Jazzy, wood-panelled café-bar serving cakes and snacks; outdoor tables front the picturesque main square.

O Soeiro

Rua Município, Alcoutim ☎281 546 241. Café Mon–Sat 9am–11pm; restaurant Mon–Fri noon–3pm. With outdoor tables on a little terrace right above the waterfront, this is a lovely spot for a drink or snack, with inexpensive lunchtime grills cooked on an outside barbecue in summer. The upstairs restaurant (lunches only) does a good range of moderately priced meals, including game and river fish such as *lampreia* (lamprey), the local specialities.

Restaurants

Alcatía

Rua de Timor 8970, Alcoutim ☎281 546 606. Tues–Sat noon–3pm & 7–10pm, Sun 7–10pm. Despite its unpromising location in a shopping centre on the way to the youth hostel, about 1km out of town, this modern restaurant offers fine local cuisine including wild boar, rabbit and hare at very reasonable prices.

Os Arcos

Avda da República 45, Vila Real ☎281 543 764. Daily 12.30–3pm & 7.30–11pm. A bustling neighbourhood restaurant serving a good range of inexpensive Portuguese nosh, including some good rice dishes, *bacalhau* and tuna from around €10. It also has an attached *pastelaria*.

Caves do Guadiana

Avda da República 89–90, Vila Real ☎281 544 498. Mon–Wed & Fri–Sun noon–4pm & 7–11pm. The best place in town for a quality meal at moderate prices. It's got a nice tiled, vaulted interior and offers a long list of fish, grilled meats and omelettes.

Churrasqueira Arenilha

Rua Cândido dos Reis, Vila Real ☎281 544 038. Daily noon–3pm & 7–10pm. This place opposite the market building has an attractive interior lined with old black-and-white photos of Vila Real. The Portuguese food includes a fine *arroz de marisco*, or go for a simple pizza.

Eira Gaio

Rua 25 de Abril, Castro Marim ☎281 351 358. Mon–Sat noon–3pm & 7–10pm, Sun noon–3pm. On the road opposite the tourist office, this rough-and-ready diner has a limited but inexpensive menu (mains under €7) with good *bacalhau* dishes.

Albufeira and around

Albufeira has long been the most popular resort in the Algarve. Its name derives from the Moorish occupation when it was called "Al-buhera", Castle of the Sea. Perched on a low clifftop overlooking a stunning beach, the historic centre is a picturesque medley of dazzling whitewashed churches and terracotta-roofed houses. Around the old centre lies an enormous swathe of development, but at least the villas, hotels, bars and restaurants that radiate for miles outwards are largely low-rise and invisible from the beach itself. If you miss your home comforts, you'll find no end of bars showing live European soccer on TV, and you're never far away from a café offering a full English breakfast.

In the vicinity, there are fine walks round the historic castle at Paderne, while Alte, set in the foothills of the Serra de Caldeirão, is one of the Algarve's prettiest and best-kept villages.

Central Albufeira

The focus of Albufeira is the **main square**, Largo Engenheiro Duarte Pacheco, a broad, pedestrianized space with a small fountain and benches beneath palm trees. But, although the surrounding buildings are traditionally Portuguese, their contents are decidedly international, mostly pizza restaurants and bars with English names. After dark, the square becomes a focus for families and promenaders, accompanied in high season by live performers and buskers.

Off the square, **Rua Candida dos Reis** permanently buzzes, by day with little craft stalls and after dark with row upon row of bars selling cheap cocktails. South of the square, Rua 5 de Outubro leads to a dramatic tunnel that has been blasted through the cliff to give access to the beach.

▼ ALBUFEIRA OLD TOWN

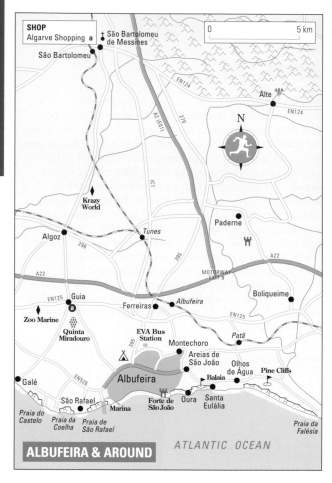

SHOP
Algarve Shopping **a**

São Bartolomeu de Messines

São Bartolomeu

0   5 km

Alte

EN124

EN124

EN124

A2 (E01)

270

IC1

Krazy World

Tunes

Paderne

Algoz

296

395

A22

A2 (E01)

A22

MOTORWAY
EXIT 9

Boliqueime

EN125

Guia **a**

Ferreiras

Albufeira

EN125

Zoo Marine

Quinta Miradouro

Patã

EVA Bus Station

Montechoro

395

Areias de São João

Olhos de Água

Pine Cliffs

Galé

EN526

Albufeira

Balaia

São Rafael

Marina

Forte de São João

Oura

Santa Eulália

Praia do Castelo

Praia da Coelha

Praia de São Rafael

Praia da Falésia

ALBUFEIRA & AROUND

ATLANTIC OCEAN

Above the tunnel, steps lead up to Praça Miguel Bombarda where you'll find two of the town's most important churches. The **Ermide de São Sebastião** has a distinctive Manueline door, though most of the building was constructed in the early eighteenth century with Baroque touches. Inside is the **Museu Arte Sacra** (July–Oct 10am–midnight; Nov–June Tues–Sun 10.30am–5pm; €1 donation), a diminutive

sacred-art museum containing plaster images of saints. Just north of here is the **Igreja de Santana**, a whitewashed eighteenth-century church with an attractive dome. From the patio at the front there are lovely views over the distinctive filigree chimneys of the old town down to the sea.

Museu Arqueológico

Trav da Bateria. Tues–Sun: mid-Sept to May 10.30am–4.30pm; June to

Visiting Albufeira

Albufeira's bus terminal is around 2km north of town. A red-route shuttle bus runs at 10 and 40 minutes past each hour (7am–midnight; until 10pm Oct–April; €1) to the top end of Avenida da Liberdade, five minutes' walk from the central square, Largo Engenheiro Duarte Pacheco. Albufeira's nearest train station is 6km north of town at Ferreiras; a bus connects it with the bus terminal every 45 minutes or so (daily 7am–8pm), or a taxi will cost about €10, depending on the time of day. Parking in the central area is a hit-and-miss affair, so you're best off following signs to out-of-town car parks.

The turismo (May–Sept Tues–Thurs 9.30am–7pm, Fri–Mon 9.30am–12.30pm & 2–6pm; Oct–April Tues–Thurs 9.30am–5.30pm, Fri–Mon 9.30am–1pm & 2–5.30pm; ☎289 585 279) is on Rua 5 de Outubro, close to the tunnel.

mid-Sept 2.30–8pm. Free. Albufeira's most interesting museum, the Museu Arqueológico, is in the former town hall. It has a rather sparse but well laid-out collection of artefacts gathered from the area and dating from Neolithic times to the present. There are fragments of mosaics from a Roman villa unearthed nearby, Visigoth rock tombs and jars, and even a Moorish silo excavated *in situ* beneath the museum. More recent remains include Manueline fragments from the old Igreja Matriz, while upstairs atmospheric black-and-white photos show the town and its beach before the advent of mass tourism.

Travessa da Bateria

Beyond the museum, Travessa da Bateria runs parallel to the beach past some of the town's most atmospheric backstreets – Rua do Cemitério Velho, Rua da Igreja Velha and Rua Nova – narrow, cobbled and lined with little cottages. At the end of Travessa da Bateria, steps wind down to the beach via the former fish market, now a favourite haunt of buskers and people just chilling out under the shady roof.

Albufeira beach

The beach fronting Albufeira is a glorious sweep of soft sand flanked by strange tooth-like rock formations and backed by a sandstone cliff. The western end of the beach can be reached via a tunnel, or via steep steps or a lift which descend the cliff below the *Hotel Rocamar*. This tends to be the busiest stretch

▼ ALBUFEIRA BEACH

PLACES

Albufeira and around

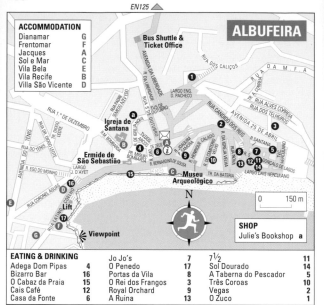

ALBUFEIRA

ACCOMMODATION
Dianamar	G
Frentomar	F
Jacques	A
Sol e Mar	C
Vila Bela	E
Vila Recife	B
Villa São Vicente	D

Bus Shuttle &
Ticket Office

Igreja de
Santana

Ermide de
São Sebastião

Museu
Arqueológico

Lift

Viewpoint

SHOP
Julie's Bookshop a

0   150 m

EATING & DRINKING
Adega Dom Pipas	4	Jo Jo's	7	7½	11
Bizarro Bar	16	O Penedo	17	Sol Dourado	14
O Cabaz da Praia	15	Portas da Vila	8	A Taberna do Pescador	5
Cais Café	12	O Rei dos Frangos	3	Três Coroas	10
Casa da Fonte	6	Royal Orchard	9	Vegas	2
		A Ruína	13	O Zuco	1

of sand, where you can hire out
pedaloes, go water-skiing, or
ride on inflatable bananas.

When the waves get up, the
eastern end of the beach, around
the jetty, is popular with surfers.
At low tide you can walk on
for another twenty minutes
or so beyond the jetty below
more low cliffs. The sands here
are backed by the odd beach
café and marginally less busy.
Take care when swimming, as
the beach becomes gradually
rockier towards the cliffs at the
far end. You can clamber on to
the low cliffs beyond here and
follow the coastal paths round
to Praia da Oura, a 45-minute
walk passing a series of natural
grottoes, rock bridges and
blowholes carved into the rock
by the sea.

Montechoro

Much of Albufeira's package
accommodation is slightly away

from the historic centre, in one
of a handful of small resort-
villages. The largest of these,
Montechoro, is a downmarket
suburb known as "the strip",
with a gaudy Eurotrashy appeal.
A toy train circles Albufeira out
to Montechoro every twenty
minutes or so from 9am to
midnight, all night in August
(€2 a trip, or €3/6 a half/full-
day pass). Alternatively, a regular
blue route bus goes from the
bus station via Areias de São
João, another resort-village,
to Montechoro (€1 a ride or
bilhete turístico day passes for €3).

Nearby, east of the centre,
lies Albufeira's bullring. The
tourist office can give details
of the weekly May-to-October
bullfights.

The marina and beaches
west of Albufeira

Reached on the red bus
route, 2km west of Albufeira,

is a modern yachting marina backed by an alarming Legoland conglomeration of brightly coloured modern houses, shops and restaurants. Daily boat trips depart from here up and down the coastline from around €15 a head.

Some of the region's best cove beaches begin a couple of kilometres to the west of Albufeira – you can walk from one to another along a clifftop path. The first of the beaches, **São Rafael**, is a lovely Blue Flag sandy cove studded with sandstone pillars and backed by low cliffs, with its own swanky restaurant. Also with a beach café-restaurant, and reached down a steep road, **Praia do Castelo** is a smaller sandy bay nestling below cliffs. Usually the quietest beach on this stretch is **Praia da Coelho**, reached via a delightful sandy track through unspoilt countryside, around a ten-minute walk from the car park. Development becomes more intense at **Praia de Galé**, where a massive sweeping swathe of sand stretches all the way west to Armação de Pêra (see p.116). Another Blue Flag beach with a cluster of hotels, cafés and restaurants, this is as good a place as any to enjoy a day on the beach.

Zoo Marine

Ⓦ www.zoomarine.com. May–June 22 & Sept 19 to end Oct daily 10am–5pm; June 23–Sept 18 daily 10am–8pm; Nov–April Tues–Sun 10am–5pm. Adults €21.50, children €13. Right on the main EN125, this part-zoo, part-theme park boasts swimming pools, fairground rides, an aquarium and animal enclosures. Various shows are staggered throughout the day, including performing parrots, sea-lion performances and a spectacular dolphin show. With inexpensive cafés into the bargain, Zoo Marine can make a pretty perfect family day out.

Krazy World

Ⓦ www.krazy-world.com. Jan–June, Sept & Oct Wed–Sun 10am–6pm; July & Aug daily 10am–7.30pm. €9.50, under-12s €4.50. Buses from Albufeira to São Bartolomeu de Messines stop near the entrance. Around 18km northwest of Albufeira is a sizeable zoo-cum-theme park, Krazy World. The

▲ KRAZY WORLD

entrance fee includes the neatly landscaped park, fairground – mostly traditional rides such as Ferris wheels and roundabouts – as well as a mini zoo, children's farm, swimming pools (summer only) and crazy golf course. Don't miss "Amazonia", a reptile zone with enormous pythons, crocodiles and a turtle city.

Paderne

Served by hourly buses from Albufeira.
The main appeal of Paderne, a traditional village set on a low hill, lies in strolling round the sloping streets and soaking up the relaxed atmosphere. Its only real sight is the parish church, which dates from 1506 – its doorway retains some fine Manueline flourishes. A worthy detour is the pleasant walk to the scant remains of a **Moorish castle**, which lie some 2km southeast of town on the road to Boliqueime. The castle is signed down a dirt track, officially labelled as a 1.4-kilometre pedestrian route, though a steady stream of cars usually bumps its way up the track to avoid the steep final ascent. Nearby motorway aside, it's a lovely walk through olive groves, accompanied by the rhythmic screech of cicadas.

At the top of the hill lie the atmospheric remains of a twelfth-century Moorish fort which commands great views of the surrounding countryside. The fort was captured by knights from the Order of Christ in 1248 during the Christian reconquest of the Algarve, and you can still see remains of the later brick fourteenth-century hermitage, the Ermida de Nossa Senhora do Castelo, inside the castle's crumbly walls.

Alte

A series of narrow cobbled streets tumbling down a hillside makes Alte one of the region's most picturesque villages, an asset well exploited by tour operators who ship in day-trippers throughout the summer. Come early or at the end of the day, however, and the place is given over to locals once more.

Alte's only sight is the graceful sixteenth-century Igreja Matriz, with a Manueline doorway, though most people spend their time wandering round the cobbled backstreets and out to a couple of natural springs or *fontes* around ten minutes' walk from the centre. The first of these, Fonte Pequena, is marked by the restaurant of the same name set in an old mill. A further five minutes' walk up a reed-filled valley lies the less manicured Fonte Grande, where the river passes an old weir lined with cafés and picnic tables set under shady trees.

Alte also holds a lively flea market on the third Thursday of every month.

Guia

Shot through by a highway, Guia nevertheless merits a stop for its renowned chicken restaurants specializing in delicious char-grilled *frango*: the

▼ PADERNE CASTLE

▲ SPRING, ALTE

best are listed below. It also has a couple of fine churches, the seventeenth-century Igreja Matriz and the Baroque Nossa Senhora da Guia, the latter sporting a particularly striking interior of sumptuous blue and white *azulejos*.

Quinta Miradouro

Mon–Fri 10am–1pm & 2–5pm. Shop free, otherwise visits by appointment €7.50, or €20–30 including transport from nearby resorts. ☎968 776 971, ⓦwww.winesvidanova.com. Just south of Algarve Shopping off the main EN125 (go past the car parks east of the shopping centre) lie the open fields of Quinta Miradouro, a.k.a Cliff Richard's wine estate. Quinta Miradouro is actually one of three farms in a wine co-operative (Cliff owns the neighbouring Quinta do Moinho) which produces the strong (13–14 percent) and increasingly respected Vida Nova wines, named after the "new life" the farms have breathed into exhausted vineyards. The co-operative has become something of a pilgrimage site for Cliff Richard fans, who can often be seen posing for photographs outside Cliff's nearby farm. Visits will appeal equally to wine buffs – they include an interesting talk about the production of wine, a look at the production methods and a tasting of some of the recent blends, which you can purchase from the shop. Come in September to catch the harvest, or November when Sir Cliff often pops in for his birthday.

Visiting Alte

Alte is poorly served by public transport, with just one bus daily from Loulé, though it is well served by summer tours and jeep safaris; ask around at the travel agents in Albufeira for details.

The turismo, which doubles as a handicrafts centre, is located on the main road just below town on the Estrada da Ponte 17 (Mon–Sat 9am–5.30pm; ☎289 478 666).

▲ QUINTA MIRADOURO

Accommodation

Alte Hotel

Moninho, near Alte ☎289 478 523, ⊛www.altehotel.com. This modern hotel is on a rural hillside some 1km out of Alte, with its own restaurant and pool, and most of the comfortable en-suite rooms have superb views. €87.

Pensão Dianamar

Rua Latino Coelho 36, Albufeira ☎289 587 801, ⊛www.dianamar.com. A very well-run Swedish-owned *pensão* in the nicest part of town, a block back from the beach. En-suite rooms come with balconies, and nice touches include dried flowers, home-made soaps and tea-making facilities. Those at the top have great sea views, as does the communal roof terrace. It does a superb Swedish breakfast including cheeses, fruit and cakes, and also hosts great mid-summer parties. €60–65.

Pensão Residencial Frentomar

Rua Latino Coelho, Albufeira ☎289 512 005, ©frentomar@gmail.com.

Simple, clean rooms on a quiet sideroad just above the steps down to the beach. Try to get one with a terrace and a sea view, though these are usually snapped up quickly. €50.

Jacques Accommodation

Rua 5 de Outubro 36, Albufeira ☎289 588 640. Set in an attractive town house on the main pedestrianized street, this offers large, airy en-suite rooms, some with balconies, although front rooms can be noisy. There's a shared terrace, and each floor has an area with a fridge and coffee-making facilities. Breakfast not included. €45.

Hotel Sol e Mar

Rua J. Bernardino de Sousa, Albufeira ☎289 580 080, ⊛grupofbarata.com. On the cliff above the tunnel to the beach, this characterless but well-equipped four-star extends down five floors right onto the beach. The balconies have a prime spot overlooking the sands, while there's also a swimming pool. Rates drop considerably out of season. €125.

Residencial Vila Bela

Rua Coronel Águas 32, Albufeira ☎ & ©289 512 101, ©ctr@mal .telepac.pt. A good-value *residencial* with rooms overlooking a small swimming pool; top ones have balconies with fine sea views. There is a pleasant patio brightened by bougainvillea. It's often booked up by tour groups and there's a minimum stay of one week in high summer. April–Oct. €75.

Estalagem Vila Joya

Praia da Galé ☎289 591 795, ⊛www.vilajoya.com. One of the Algarve's most exclusive "gourmet" hotels, with a renowned double-Michelin-starred restaurant downstairs (featuring an à la carte lunch menu and evening *degustacion* menu). The pseudo-Moorish hotel has its own pool right above the beach. There are just twelve luxurious rooms and five suites. €430.

Residencial Vila Recife

Rua Miguel Bombarda 12, Albufeira ⊕289 583 740, ⊜vila.recife @sapo.pt. A huge, rambling old town house complete with its own garden and small pool. The rooms are smallish but comfortable with en-suite facilities, some with seaviews, and the *azulejos*-lined communal areas are spotless. The garden bar, complete with ceiling fans and snooker table, has live music most nights. April–Oct. €80.

Villa São Vicente Hotel

Largo Jacinto D'Ayet 4, Albufeira ⊕289 583 700, ⓌHotel-vila-sao-vicente.com. A tasteful modern three-star with tiled floors and whitewashed walls. It has its own small pool and a terrace facing the beach. Rooms facing the street are cheaper, but it's worth paying €20 extra for sea views. All rooms are en suite with TVs and a/c. €110.

Campsite

Parque de Campismo

Estrada de Ferreiras, Albufeira ⊕289 587 629, ⊜campingalbufeira@mail .telepac.pt. The finely appointed local campsite, complete with swimming pools, restaurants, bars, shops and tennis courts, is 2km to the north of town, off the N396, with regular bus connections to town (any bus to Ferreiras passes it), though space can be at a premium in high season – book ahead if possible.

Shops

Algarve Shopping

EN125, Guia. Daily: shops 10am–10pm, centre 9am–midnight. Ⓦwww .algarveshopping.pt. Giant shopping and entertainment complex just east of Guia on the main EN125. International and local stores include Zara, Massimo Dutti and Benetton, and there are plenty of cafés and restaurants on the top floor plus a multiplex cinema.

Albufeira gypsy market

Caliços (north of the centre). 1st & 3rd Tues of each month, 9am–1pm. This lively flea market is a good place to pick up inexpensive clothes and ceramics. A smaller, daily clothes market sets up at the north end of Avenida da Liberdade.

Cafés

Água Mel

Alte. Mon–Fri 9.30am–5.30pm, Sat–Sun 9.30am–7pm. An alluring café with a back balcony commanding superb vistas. The counter is equally inviting, stuffed with home-made pastries, preserves and cakes.

Cais Café

Cais Herculano, Albufeira. Daily 8am–midnight. An aromatic café offering a fine selection of tempting pastries and refreshing home-made ice creams.

Restaurants

Adega Dom Pipas

Trav dos Arcos 88, Albufeira ⊕289 588 091. Mon & Wed–Sun 11am–3pm & 6.30pm–midnight. A decent little backstreet tavern with outdoor tables on an attractive narrow alley usually strung with coloured ribbons. Go for the *bacalhau* dishes or fine grilled prawns.

Casa da Fonte

Rua João de Deus 7, Albufeira ☎289 514 578. Daily noon–3pm & 7pm–midnight. This popular restaurant is set round a beautiful Moorish-style courtyard complete with *azulejos* and a giant lemon tree. The courtyard tables fill up fast, though the interior is also attractive. Garlic prawns and mains from €9 are superb.

Fonte Pequena

Fonte Pequena, Alte ☎289 478 509. Tues–Sun noon–5.30pm; May–Sept also open Wed 7–10.30pm. A large rustic-style grill house with wooden benches laid out on a shady terrace facing the water at the *fonte*. Good regional dishes are available such as bean and meat stew or peas with poached egg and sausage. In summer, there's a barbecue night with live folk music on Wednesdays. Count on around €20 for a full meal.

O Penedo

Rua Latino Coelho, Albufeira ☎289 587 429. Daily 11am–11pm. With tasteful decor and a terrific back terrace overlooking the beach, *O Penedo* is worth seeking out. The usual Portuguese flavours are joined by some unusual combinations such as salad with stir-fried pork and chicken with Gorgonzola sauce. Mains cost €9–14.

Ramires

Rua 25 de Abril 14, Guia ☎289 561 232. Daily noon–10pm. This claims to be the first place in Guia to serve chicken piri-piri, and it is certainly expert at it – there's a lively downstairs area and an airy upstairs dining room. Mains from under €10.

O Rei dos Frangos

Trav dos Telheiros 4, Albufeira ☎289 512 981. Daily noon–3.30pm & 6pm–midnight. A first-rate little *churrasqueira* – the chicken comes smothered in piri-piri and there's also grilled steak, swordfish and a speciality meat *cataplana*. Unglamorous but good value.

Royal Orchid

Beco Bernardino de Sousa, Albufeira ☎289 502 505. Daily: May–Sept noon–2pm & 5pm–1am; Oct–April 5pm–midnight. This moderately priced Thai restaurant has sumptuous oriental decor and tables laid out in a tranquil leafy courtyard. The long menu features noodle and rice dishes with fish, meat or seafood for around €12, plus less expensive vegetarian options.

A Ruina

Largo Cais Herculano, Albufeira ☎289 512 094. Daily 12.30–3pm & 7–11pm. A superb, high-profile restaurant set in the cliffs behind the beach, specializing in fresh fish. The lower area is the best place for those with kids, as they can play in the sand while you eat. There are also two floors inside and a roof terrace. Sardines and salad make an inexpensive lunch, but otherwise you're looking at €20 per person and up.

A Taberna do Pescador

Trav Cais Herculano, Albufeira ☎289 589 196. Daily noon–3pm & 6–11pm. Recently smartened up, this remains a well-priced fish and seafood restaurant (main courses around €13); portions are huge; wash it all down with the house sangria.

Teodósio

Algoz road out of Guia ☎ 289 561 318.
Daily noon–3pm & 6.30–10.30pm.
You'll need a car to reach this
giant place, around 1km from
central Guia, but its popularity
is clear from the hordes who
come here. It is one of Guia's
most famous places for grilled
chicken, and though the interior
is unglamorous, it is certainly
buzzing, and the chicken – with
or without piri-piri – is both
delicious and a bargain (full
meals around €12).

Três Coroas

Rua do Correiro Velho 8, Albufeira
☎ 289 512 640. Daily noon–3pm &
6.30–11pm. A tranquil place with
a leafy terrace with sea views and
a small aviary in one corner. The
menu features decently priced
fish and meat dishes from €9.

O Zuco

Trav do Malpique 6, Albufeira ☎ 289 588
768. Mon, Tues & Thurs–Sun noon–3pm
& 7–10pm. A stone's throw from
the international fare of the main
square but delightfully local,
with down-to-earth grills and
usually a line of workers at the
bar. Specialities include filling
bife à Zuco steaks, casa de porco
alentejana (pork with clams) and a
challenging Sunday cozido stew.

Bars and clubs

7½

Rua São Gonçalo de Lagos 5, Albufeira.
Daily 9.30pm–3am. A fairly sedate
café-bar by day, serving light
meals, which turns into a dance
bar after dark. Karaoke sessions
and guest DJs sometimes feature.

Bizarro Bar

Esplanada Dr. Frutuosa Silva 30,
Albufeira. Mon–Sat 9am–1am. This is
a laid-back bar in a traditional,
blue-faced building high above
the eastern end of the beach,
with superb views over the
sands from its front terrace.

Jo Jo's

Rua São Gonçalo de Lagos 1, Albufeira.
Mon–Sat 10am–2am, Sun noon–2am.
A friendly family-run pub with
British soccer and other sports
on satellite TV. It also serves
pub-style food, which always
includes a vegetarian option.
The owner proudly remembers
the day Paul Gascoigne and his
mates got hopelessly drunk here.

Kiss

Rua Vasco da Gama, Areias de São
João, Albufeira. May–Sept daily
11pm–6am; Oct–April Sat & Sun
11pm–6am. Out of town, at the
southern end of Montechoro
near the Forte de São João,
this is regarded as the best
club around town, and often
hosts guest DJs. With five bars
and two dance floors there's
usually space; watch for posters
advertising events. Green and
blue bus routes pass nearby, or a
taxi costs around €8.

Portas da Vila

Rua da Bateria, Albufeira. Daily
1pm–1am. Built on the site of the
former town gates, this high-
ceilinged, traditionally decked-out
bar lies just above the old fish
market, with a few outdoor
tables on the pedestrianized steps.
The menu features a long list of
cocktails and sangria.

Vegas

Rua Candido dos Reis 22–26, Albufeira.
Daily 10am–3am. Typical of the
places on this street, this café-
cum-pub/club serves milkshakes
and coffee by day and cocktails
by night, when live soccer
on big screens gives way to
thumping music.

Armação de Pêra and around

Armação de Pêra is one of the Algarve's most popular summer retreats for Portuguese holidaymakers, a bustling high-rise resort at the western end of a fantastic sweep of sand. The 10km or so of coast between Armação de Pêra and Centianes is flat and scrubby, fronting a series of delightful cove beaches that have somehow escaped any large-scale development. The relative inaccessibility of these beaches thins out the crowds, and they are conveniently linked by a fine clifftop coastal path. There are inland attractions, too, in the form of the pottery centre at Porches and the Aqualand water park.

Armação de Pêra

Armação de Pêra is a major resort facing one of the longest beaches in the Algarve. The kernel of old buildings and the narrow, cobbled backstreets around the Praia dos Pescadores (Fishermen's Beach) are highly attractive, reminders of the time when fishermen from the village of Pêra, a couple of kilometres inland, used the once undeveloped beach to launch their *armação* – a combined fishing boat netting system.

The rest of Armação de Pêra is a characterless grid of ugly high-rises, with plenty more under construction. But stick to the beach and gardens – with its children's play area and cafés – and it is easy to ignore the modern excesses. The remains of the town's fortified walls are at the eastern end of the seafront road, where a terrace in front of a little white chapel provides sweeping views. In summer, boat trips leave from Praia dos Pescadores to explore the area's

▲ PROMENADE GARDENS, ARMAÇÃO DE PÊRA

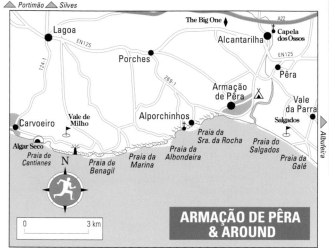

Portimão △ Silves

Lagoa
EN125
124.1
Porches
269.1
Carvoeiro
Vale de Milho
Alporchinhos
Algar Seco
Praia de Centianes
N
Praia de Benagil
Praia da Marina
Praia da Albondeira
Praia da Sra. da Rocha
Armação de Pêra
Alcantarilha
Capela dos Ossos
EN125
A22
The Big One
Pêra
Vale da Parra
Salgados
Praia do Salgados
Praia da Galé

0   3 km

ARMAÇÃO DE PÊRA & AROUND

Albufeira

fine caves and unusual rock formations to the west around Praia da Senhora da Rocha (around €15 per person).

Alcantarilha

Alcantarilha is a surprisingly unspoilt town, considering its position on the EN125. Its main sight is its eighteenth-century Igreja Matriz, which contains a Capela dos Ossos, a chapel lined with the bones of around 1500 humans, similar to that in Faro (see p.54). These chapels were partly a practical solution to lack of cemetery space. Unfortunately the chapel opens only occasionally, though at such times entry is free.

Aqualand

ⓦwww.aqualand.pt. Late May to Sept daily 10am–6pm. €17.50, children under 10 €14.50. Beyond Alcantarilha just off the EN125, the Aqualand is a giant water park set among lawns and palms, with an array of pools and slides with apt names such as "Labyrinth", "Crazy leap" and "Kamikaze". Best of all is the "Banzai Boggan", a terrifying 23-metre, near-vertical slide into water.

Porches

The pleasant if unexceptional village of Porches is famous for its hand-painted pottery (majolica). The chunky majolica-ware employs glazing techniques used since Moorish times. Workshops – usually open daily – line the main EN125,

---

Visiting Armação de Pêra

Armação de Pêra's bus terminal (☎282 315 781) is at the eastern end of the town and there are regular services from Albufeira, Portimão and Silves. The helpful turismo is on the seafront Avenida Marginal, ten minutes from the bus station (May–Sept Tues–Thurs 9.30am–7pm, Fri–Mon 9.30am–12.30pm & 2–6pm; Oct–April Tues–Thurs 9.30am–5.30pm, Fri–Mon 9.30am–1pm & 2–5.30pm; ☎282 312 145). A land train also trundles round town out to the campsite roughly hourly (10am–midnight, €4).

although not all the goods on sale are produced in Porches; you can find everything from Barcelos pots from northern Portugal to wood-burning ovens and *azulejos*-inlaid table tops, which can be shipped abroad if required. A good place to browse is Casa Algarve (daily 9.30am–6.30pm), just west of Porches, set in a late nineteenth-century former restaurant with an *azulejo*-lined back patio.

Praia da Albondeira and Praia da Marinha

Occasional buses from Lagoa; by car, turn south off the EN125, between Porches and Lagoa, opposite the International School. The attractive beach of Praia da Albondeira marks the start of a superb ninety-minute coastal footpath which stretches west for 4km all the way to the pretty village of Benagil (see below). Look out for bizarre *Algares*, giant

(mostly fenced off) potholes the depth of three-storey houses, naturally eroded into the limestone. The path heads past the alluring Praia da Marinha, nestling below a craggy red sandstone cliff, with the only trace of development being a tasteful villa complex a little up the hill. To reach the beach from the neatly tended car park, descend the cobbled track that leads off to the left from the clifftop picnic tables. The beach has a simple seasonal café-restaurant.

Benagil

Benagil is a tiny fishing village with a cluster of buildings above a narrow gully. The road loops down over a dried-up river valley, at the bottom of which, under high cliffs, is a fine beach dotted with fishing boats. Ask around and the fishermen are usually happy to take you out to see an amazing sea cave, as

big as a cathedral, with a hole in its roof, for around €15 per person. You can walk to the top of the cave on the path that starts by the restaurant *Algar* just east of the village; take care, as there are deep drops.

Praia de Centianes

Reached by a lengthy set of steps, Praia de Centianes, to the west of Benagil, is a fine beach set below sculpted cliffs, with its own café-restaurant right on the sands. However, as it's backed by a fair amount of development, the sands can get very crowded in high season.

▲ PRAIA DA MARINHA

▲ BENAGIL

Accommodation

Hotel Garbe
Avda Beira Mar 1, Armação de Pêra
☎282 320 260, ✆hotelgarbe.com.
A few minutes' walk west of
the tourist office, this modern
block enjoys a prime site facing
the beach. Rooms are varied,
although most have balconies.
The hotel also has a pool, TV
and games room, in-house
Indian restaurant and a babysitting service. €190, or €225
for sea views.

Rosamar
Rua Dom João II, Armação de Pêra
☎282 312 377, ✉paraizo@gawab
.com. If you don't mind high-rise
living, the spacious apartments
here, a block back from the
seafront, are good value. Each has
a sitting room, kitchenette and
heavy Portuguese decor; the best
have sea-facing balconies. No
breakfast, but there is a bar. €90.

Vila Linda Mar
Benagil ☎282 342 331,
✆vilalindamar.com. In a rural
setting 1km east of Benagil,
Vila Linda Mar is a tasteful,
traditionally decorated
guesthouse with its own lawns
and a small pool. There are just
a handful of rooms, all with
bathrooms, TVs and fridges; the
best ones with balconies offer
distant sea views. It also has a
fine restaurant (see p.122). €80,
or €105 for sea views.

Campsite

Parque de Campismo
Armação de Pêra ☎282 312 904,
✆www.roteiro-campista.pt. Around
1km north of town, facing
a marshy lagoon, this well-
equipped campsite has its own
pool, supermarket, restaurant
and gardens.

Cafés

Esplanade Bar Mini Golf
Avda Marginal, Armação de Pêra
☎282 312 414. Mon, Tues & Thurs–
Sun 8am–10pm. Near the tourist
office, with outside tables on a

terrace overlooking the beach. The perfect place to watch the sun go down over a Superbock or two, or, if this is too sedate, there's an outdoor games area complete with children's rides, table football and minigolf.

Restaurants

Casa Lamy
Benagil ☎282 359 839. Tues–Sun 10am–10pm. Above the beach to the west, this has a great little terrace and cosy interior. Fine fresh fish and chicken piri-piri, and the prawns with garlic are hard to beat. Mains from €10.

Estrela do Mar
Largo 25 de Abril, Armação de Pêra ☎282 313 775. Tues–Sun 11am–3pm & 6pm–midnight. Right on the fishermen's beach nestled among the boats, this simple beach shack offers bargain Portuguese staples (under €15 for a full meal); the *sardinhas assada* (grilled sardines) are superb, or try the filling *feijoada de camaráo* (prawn and bean stew).

Rocha da Palha
Rua N.S. dos Navegantes, Armação de Pêra ☎282 315 596. Daily 11am–3pm & 7–11pm. With tables on decking facing the sands, this is a smart but surprisingly reasonable restaurant with mains from around €10. Service is crisp and the fish, grills and daily specials are usually superb.

O Serol
Rua Portas do Mar 2, Armação de Pêra ☎282 312 146. Mon, Tues & Thurs–Sun noon–3.30pm & 6–10.30pm. Just east of the church near the fishermen's beach, with a cosy interior and an outdoor terrace, this is one of the town's best and not too pricey fish restaurants (€15–20 for a full meal), full of trussed lobsters and crabs. It also lets out inexpensive rooms.

Vila Linda Mar
Benagil ☎282 342 331. Mon & Wed–Sun 7–10.30pm. A rural hotel 1km east of Benagil, where local chef Captain Carlos cooks superb set meals most evenings (open to non-residents, though it's best to book in advance). For €18, meals include a fine range of starters followed by meat or fish, all using traditional recipes and organic ingredients.

Carvoeiro and around

The former fishing village of **Carvoeiro** has developed into a firm favourite for package holidays, and its centre of fishermen's houses spilling down a hillside to the beach is surrounded by substantial development. Out of season the town has more appeal, and it is within easy reach of the Slide and Splash water park. Some of the region's finest cove beaches can be found on the less developed coastline between Carvoeiro and Ferragudo, another attractive former fishing village on the Rio Arade estuary. However, bear in mind that there is limited public transport to these beaches, so you'll need a car to reach them.

Carvoeiro

Cut into the red cliffs and clustered round a sandy cove, Carvoeiro was once one of the Algarve's prettiest fishing villages. Today it has grown into a somewhat rambling resort and its beach struggles to cope with the summer crowds, but, with a plethora of cafés and restaurants and a busy nightlife, it's anything but dull.

Algar Seco

One kilometre east from Carvoeiro along the coast road are the impressive rock formations of Algar Seco,

where steps down the cliffs pass sculpted rocks, pillars and blowholes above slapping waves. There's a small café-bar, *Boneca* (March–Sept daily 10am–dusk), which is named after the neighbouring A Boneca, a rock window reached through a short tunnel, offering neatly framed sea views. Boat trips from Portimão (see p.133) often stop off here.

▲ CARVOEIRO

▲ ALGAR SECO

of Praia da Caneiros sits below cliffs and has soft sand and a smart café-restaurant. Just off the beach stands a rock stack known as Leixão das Gaivotas, usually flecked with rows of basking cormorants.

Praia Pintadinho
Praia Pintadinho is a lovely cliff-backed cove beach, with its own café-restaurant. The sandy cove has rock caves at either end where you can shelter from the sun. Scramble up the rocks to the east of the bay and there are some fine clifftop walks along the coast; within five minutes you reach a small lighthouse, with views to Ponta da Piedade to the west and, on clear days, as far as the Sagres peninsula.

Slide and Splash
Vale de Deus, signposted off the EN125. Served by 1–2 daily buses from most nearby resorts, including Carvoeiro, Albufeira and Armação de Pêra. ☏282 341 685, ⓦwww.slidesplash.com. Daily April–Oct 10am–5pm (until 6pm in July). €16, children €13. For a change from the beach, the water chutes, flumes, slides, pools and aquatic fun at the Slide & Splash theme park make a great half-day outing, especially for older kids.

Praia da Caneiros
Regular buses from Portimão via Ferragudo. The idyllic cove beach

Praia Grande
Praia Grande lies within Portimão's harbour walls, on the opposite side of the estuary to the town. The western end of this fine stretch of broad sands (Praia Grande means "big beach") is dotted with restaurants; the eastern end is quieter.

Ferragudo
Regular buses from Portimão. Ferragudo, facing Portimão

Visiting Carvoeiro
Regular buses call at Carvoeiro from Portimão and Armação de Pêra, though some involve a change at Lagoa. The turismo (May–Sept Tues–Thurs 9.30am–7pm, Fri–Mon 9.30am–12.30pm & 2–6pm; Oct–April Tues–Thurs 9.30am–5.30pm, Fri–Mon 9.30am–1pm & 2–5.30pm; ☏282 357 728), just behind the beach, can give details of private rooms. A toy train passes round town and out to Algar Seco and Praia de Centianes (see p.118) every twenty minutes (May–Sept only, €4 round trip).

across the estuary, is one of the least spoilt former fishing villages on this stretch of the Algarve. Although many of the old fishermen's cottages have been snapped up by wealthy Lisboans and expats, few concessions have been made to international tourism and the village retains its traditional character. The town spreads round a strip of palm-fringed gardens running alongside a narrow riverlet up to the cobbled main square, Praça Rainha Dona Leonor. Just west of here, the riverlet ends at the Rio Arade estuary, where a promenade skirts a small fishing harbour and a row of fish restaurants. South of here, a warren of atmospheric cobbled backstreets winds its way up the side of a hill to the town's church, parts of which date back to the fourteenth century; there are great views over the estuary to Portimão from the church terrace. At the foot of the hill below the church – accessible at low tide from the fishing harbour or by taking the road that skirts the old town – lies the town beach, Angrinha, a thin stretch of sand which gets progressively more appealing as it approaches the **Castelo de São João do Arade**. The sixteenth-century fort, one of a pair built to defend the Rio

Arade (the other is opposite in Praia da Rocha, see p.134), sits impressively right on the sands. Remodelled in the early twentieth century by the poet Coelho Carvalho, it is currently in private hands.

Accommodation

Algar Seco Parque

Rua das Flores, Algar Seco ☎282 350 440, ⓦwww.algarseco.pt. A series of tasteful studios, apartments and villas spills down terraced gardens above the Algar Seco rocks. There are pools, a bar and restaurant, and each room is well equipped and tastefully furnished in traditional Portuguese stye. Studios from €125.

Hotel Carvoeiro Sol

Carvoeiro ☎282 357 301, ⓦcarvoeirosol.com. A comfortable, if unimaginative, four-star concrete block right by the beach. Rooms come with small balconies, though you pay around €26 extra for sea views. There's also a pool, courtyard bar and a babysitting service. €152.

Casabela Hotel

Praia Grande ☎282 490 650, ⓦwww .hotel-casabela.com. Well worth a splurge, the *Casabela Hotel* is set in a low modern building with

▼ FERRAGUDO

fantastic grounds above Praia Grande and a short walk from Praia Pintadinho. Most rooms have wonderful views, and there's a heated pool, bar, tennis courts and disabled access. €185.

O Castelo

Rua da Casino 59–61, Carvoeiro ☎ & ☎282 357 416, ✉casteloguesthouse @clix.pt. Overlooking the beach, five minutes' walk uphill from the tourist office, this is the budget option in town, but book ahead as there are just three rooms. Each is clean and modern with superb views; two have their own balconies. The price does not include breakfast. €50.

Quinta da Horta

Rua do Regato, Ferragudo ☎913 360 738, ⊛naturist-holidays-portugal .com. Around 1km east of town, this charming "clothes optional" place is run by a British artist who also runs art courses – and the occasional naturist gathering. A series of tasteful spartan rooms and a self-catering apartment (sleeps four) are set round a tropical garden with a small pond. There's a little plunge pool, a sauna, TV room and tennis court, and three horses for treks or for picnics in a gypsy cart. A superb organic breakfast is included in the price. €70.

Vila Castelo

Angrinha, Apartado 33, Ferragudo ☎282 461 993, UK bookings on ☎01604 584888, ⊛www.vilacastelo.com. A modern, British-run upmarket apartment complex on the hillside opposite the castle, a five-minute walk from the old town church. Apartments are well equipped with smart kitchens and satellite TV; the best ones have balconies or terraces with superb views over the castle.

There's also a communal pool. One-week minimum let in high season. €110.

Campsite

Parque Campismo de Ferragudo

☎282 461 121, ⊛www.roteiro -campista.pt. This privately run campsite, 3km east of Ferragudo between Praia Pintadinho and Praia da Caneiros, is only open to those with an International Camping Carnet. It's very well equipped with a pool, kids' play area, large supermarket and a restaurant. There's usually plenty of space for tents beneath the trees.

Cafés

Gelataria Marina

Praça Rainha D. Leonor 12–13, Ferragudo. Daily 8am–11pm, June–Sept until midnight. Filled with families at weekends, this is the best spot for ice cream and pastries; sunny seats spill out onto the square.

Restaurants

O Barco

Largo da Praia, Carvoeiro ☎282 357 975. Mon, Tues & Thurs–Sun 10am–midnight. Unexceptional, reasonably priced food – from snacks to Portuguese dishes and pasta from around €9 – with an excellent position facing the sands.

O Barril

Trav do Caldeirão 1–5, Ferragudo ☎282 461 215. Mon & Wed–Sun noon–2pm & 7pm–2am. Tucked under the arches in an alley just off the main square, this bar-restaurant serves pricey seafood and fish, but it does offer live Fado sessions most nights from 8pm and the lobster is hard to fault. Over €20 for a meal.

A Fonte

Escadinhas do Vai-Assar 10, Carvoeiro ☎282 356 707. Daily noon–2.30pm & 6–10.30pm. Just west of the main street into town, this has more character than most of Carvoeiro's restaurants, with tasty meat and fish from €10, large salads and a fine speciality, *arroz de tamboril* (monkfish rice). A few tables spill out onto a small side alley.

Pintadinho

Praia Pintadinho ☎282 461 659. Late March to Oct daily 10am–dusk (until midnight in July & Aug). This simple beachside café-restaurant sits right on the sands; snacks and drinks are well priced but seafood and fish, though tasty, are expensive. The wonderful sea views, however, make it all worthwhile.

Rei das Praias

Praia da Caneiros ☎282 461 006. March–Oct daily 10am–10pm. On stilts above the beach, this is rated as one of the Algarve's best beachside restaurants, with meals served either on the terrace or in the swish interior. There is a fine wine list, and expensive but superb dishes include prawns cooked in piri-piri sauce and fish baked in salt. Upwards of €20 for a full meal.

A Ria

Rua Infante Santo 27, Ferragudo ☎282 451 790. Tues–Sun noon–3pm & 7pm–midnight. A small, friendly restaurant with good-value fish and grills and a wide array of rice dishes including tasty *arroz de polvo* (octopus rice) – a full meal

will cost around €15. It's one of the first places you come to along the main harbour front, with an outdoor grill at the front.

Sueste

Rua da Ribeira 91, Ferragudo ☎282 461 592. Tues–Sun 12.30–3pm & 7–11pm. The most arty and buzzy of a row of fish restaurants facing the harbour. Superior if pricey (€20 plus for a meal) fish dishes are served on an outdoor terrace or in a cosy interior.

O Velho Novo

Rua Manuel Teixeira Gomes 2, Ferragudo. Daily 6pm–midnight. Five minutes' walk from the main square – cross the rivulet along the road signed to Belavista and it's on the left – this good-value option offers fish, seafood and meats grilled on an outside barbecue. You can eat at tables inside or sit out on wooden benches; full meals cost under €15.

Bars

La Be

Rua Vasco da Gama 33, Ferragudo. Mon, Tues, Thurs, Fri & Sun 8pm–4am, Sat 5pm–4am. One of Ferragudo's livelier bars, with pub-like decor – you can't miss the Egyptian-inspired murals on the outside.

Clubs

Bote Disco Club

Largo do Carvoeiro, Carvoeiro ☎282 357 285. June–Sept Tues–Sun 8pm–6am; Oct–May Fri & Sat only. A lively and fun nightclub on a prime coastal spot, with a beach-facing terrace for a breather between the contemporary sounds. Minimum consumption of around €10.

Silves and around

Surrounded by orange groves and dominated by a Moorish castle, Silves is the Algarve's most enticing inland town. Under the Moors, Silves, then called Xelb, was capital of the al-Gharb and had a population three times the current one, though many of its finer buildings were destroyed in the earthquake of 1755. Today it is a pleasant market town, with a series of bustling cobbled streets leading up from the riverfront to the small, leafy, central square, Praça do Município. Alongside, the Torreão das Portas da Cidade – the remains of the Moorish town gate – mark the extent of the oldest parts of town, which is dominated by the cathedral and the imposing fortress. Silves sits in the heart of some picturesque countryside, best enjoyed at the reservoir, Barragem do Arade.

The old town

Down on the riverfront, near the narrow thirteenth-century bridge, Silves' market (Mon–Sat 8am–1pm) has some fine outdoor grill-cafés (see p.130)

▼ HEADING UP TO THE SÉ, SILVES

SILVES & AROUND

0   5 km

N

Barragem de Arade

Santo Estêvão

Quinta do Rio

EN124

Cruz de Portugal

Silves

Rio Arade

Silves Gare

where you can sit and watch life go by. The river valley opposite is still cultivated, the fields dotted with fragrant orange trees. Most of the old town uphill from here is pedestrianized as far as the leafy Largo do Município. On the square a small exhibitions room, **Caminho do Gharb** (Mon–Fri 9am–5pm), traces the town's Islamic heritage (see box p.128) through maps, projections and artefacts.

Visiting Silves

The train station lies 2km south of town; there are usually connecting buses. Arriving by bus, you'll be dropped on the main road at the foot of the town near the riverfront, next to the market. During the summer, regular boat trips pass up the Rio Arade to Silves from Portimão; see p.133.

The turismo is at Rua 25 de Abril 26–28 (Mon–Fri: May–Sept 9.30am–12.30pm & 2–6pm; Oct–April 9.30am–1pm & 2–5.30pm; ☎282 442 255) and can give out details of local events, including the Medieval Fair in August, when the town is visited by jugglers and acrobats in thirteenth-century garb.

The fortress

Daily: July & Aug 9am–8pm; Sept–June 9am–5.30pm; last entry 30min before closing time. €1.25, under-12s free.

The Moorish fortress remains the focal point of Silves with an impressively complete set of sandstone walls and towers. It is currently undergoing extensive renovation, and plans include the re-creation of a Moorish-style garden, a traditional well and the governor's palace; work is scheduled to finish in 2008. Renovation also restricts access to the wonderful vaulted thirteenth-century water cistern, the Cisterna Grande, that once served the town. Some 10m in height and supported by six columns, the cistern is said to be haunted by a Moorish maiden who can be seen sailing across the underground waters during a full moon.

The Sé

Mon–Sat 9am–noon & 1–5.30pm, Sun limited hours between Mass. Free.

Sited below the fortress, Silves' cathedral, or Sé, is an impressive thirteenth-century edifice built on the site of the Grand Mosque. Between 1242 and 1577, this was the Algarve's most important church, but the bishopric was moved to Faro when Silves lost its role as a major port. Flanked by broad Gothic towers, it has a suitably defiant, military appearance, though the Great Earthquake and poor restoration since have left the interior less impressive than the exterior. The tombs lining the cathedral walls are of bishops and of Crusaders who died taking Silves back from the Moors.

Opposite the Sé is the newer Igreja da Misericórdia (same hours as cathedral; free), a sixteenth-century church with a fine Manueline doorway and hung with seven impressive religious images, painted on wood. It also hosts temporary exhibitions.

Museu Arqueologia

Rua da Porta de Loulé. Mon–Sat 9am–5.30pm. €1.50. Despite a lack of English-language labelling, the archeological museum is an

▲ THE SÉ, SILVES

EATING & DRINKING
Casa Velha	3
Inglês	1
Marisqueira Rui	4
U Monchiqueiro	5
Rosa	2

ACCOMMODATION
| Colina dos Mouros | B |
| Sousa | A |

▽ Station & A22

engaging collection, containing various remains from Silves and the surrounding area. There are Stone Age pillars, Roman pots and coins and beautiful Moorish and later Portuguese ceramics. Upstairs, the temporary exhibition hall offers a great vantage point from which to view the ten-metre-deep Moorish well, left *in situ* in the basement. You can also go out onto parts of the old town walls, which offer fine views over the town.

Fábrica do Inglês

Rua Gregório Mascarenhas. ⓦwww .fabrica-do-ingles.com. Free except during special events, when hours and charges vary. The Fábrica do Inglês (English Factory) is an exhibition centre-cum-theme park set in a former cork factory, opened in 1894 by a three-man team from Catalonia, Silves and England (hence the name). A series of cafés and bars is clustered round a delightful central courtyard filled with outdoor tables below scented orange trees. It is most animated when it hosts the annual summer **Silves Beer Festival**, usually in July, and on Friday nights when there are often special events, including sound and light shows. It also incorporates the **Museu da Cortiça** (Mon–Sun 9.30am–1pm & 2–5.30pm; €2), a small cork museum. There are a few evocative black-and-white

Moorish Silves

Under the Moors, Silves was a thriving port and a place of grandeur, described in contemporary accounts as being "of shining brightness" within its three dark circuits of guarding walls. It was also famed for its artistic community, and in the tenth century it was considered culturally more important than Granada, the leading Moorish city in Spain. Its greatness largely ended in 1189, with the arrival of Sancho I at the head of a mixed army of Crusaders, and Silves permanently fell to Christian forces in 1249. The gradual silting up of the Rio Arade over the next few centuries ended Silves' role as one of the great cultural centres of Iberia.

Golf and the environment

There are currently plans to build up to four golf courses in the area around Silves, fuelling a heated debate about the sustainability of such a water-guzzling sport in the face of global warming. The pro-golf lobby call golf "the snow of the Algarve", attracting well-heeled visitors to the region especially outside the summer months. They also argue that courses offer areas of wilderness and lakes that are ideal for wildlife, and that the upmarket resorts accompanying them are less intensive than large-scale package development. They also provide jobs: a golf course employs up to a hundred staff, while a farmer in a similar area would employ half a dozen at most.

Environmentalists, however, are worried. The Algarve's current golf courses already use the equivalent amount of water used by sixty percent of the population, while overuse of boreholes can lead to salination and contamination of drinking supplies. Although some courses use recycled water for irrigation, fertilizers and pesticides used to keep the greens weed-free are environmentally harmful. Meanwhile, traditional, relatively environmentally friendly mixed agricultural systems risk being abandoned if land can be sold off to golf developers. For the time being though, it seems the environmentalists are losing the battle, as plans continue to expand the number of courses in the region from around thirty to fifty over the next few years.

photos of local cork cutters, but unless you have a keen interest in the cork industry, it's unlikely to set your pulse racing.

Barragem do Arade

Set in tranquil woodland, the Barragem do Arade is a popular spot with campervanners and birdwatchers, though you'll need your own transport to get here. There are various *barragems*, or reservoirs, dotted round the Algarve, and this is one of the area's main sources of water set amongst rolling, tree-lined hills. It's a bucolic spot popular with migrating birds, though when the water level falls in summer the barren sides of the exposed mountains spoil the picturesque effect.

Accommodation

Hotel Colina dos Mouros

Silves ☎ 282 440 420, ✉ colinadosmouros@hotmail .com. The most comfortable accommodation in town, in a modern hotel over the bridge from the fortress. Most of the pleasant rooms have fine views over Silves, and there's an outdoor pool in the small, tranquil grounds. €80.

Quinta do Rio

Sitio São Estevão, Apartado 217 ☎ & ⊕ 282 445 528. Around 5km out of Silves, off the road to São Bartolomeu de Messines, this country inn has six delightful, rustic-style rooms with passionflower-shaded terraces facing open country. Breakfast consists of fresh fruit grown on the farm, and the Italian owners can supply evening meals on request. €55.

▼ BARRAGEM DO ARADE

▲ GRILLED CHICKEN AT THE MARKETSIDE RESTAURANTS

Residencial Sousa

Rua Samora Barros 17, Silves
℡282 442 502. Characterful, if
plain, faded rooms with shared
bathrooms in an attractive town
house a couple of blocks up from
the riverfront. No breakfast. €40.

Cafés

Café Inglês

Escadas do Castelo, Silves. Mon
9am–5pm, Tues–Sun 9am–1am. A
beautifully done-up 1900s town
house with a back terrace and
tables on the cobbles outside.
Choose from moderately priced
drinks and snacks and full meals.
On Friday and Saturday nights
there's often live Latin American
or jazz music, while from June
to September the roof terrace
opens for pizzas. It also hosts
occasional art exhibitions.

Pastelaria Rosa

Largo do Município, Silves. Daily
8am–11pm. A superb old *pastelaria*
with cool interior stone walls
covered in *azulejos* and a
counter groaning with cakes
and goodies. Outdoor tables
spill onto the pretty main square
next to the fountain.

Restaurants

Casa Velha

Rua 25 de Abril 13, Silves ℡282 445
491. Daily noon–3pm & 7–11pm.
In a lovely old building near
the tourist office, this spacious
restaurant serves a range of well-
priced meat, fish and seafood
– the latter kept in bubbling
tanks. Mains from €7.

Marisqueira Rui

Rua Comendador Vilarinho 27, Silves
℡282 442 682. Mon & Wed–Sun
noon–3pm & 7–10pm. Despite its
inland position and humble
appearance, this is one of
the Algarve's best seafood
restaurants, though you can eat
a full meal for under €20. It's
very popular, so arrive early to
guarantee a table.

U Monchiqueiro

Mercado, Silves. Mon, Tues & Thurs–
Sun noon–3pm & 7–11pm. The best
of a handful of inexpensive
grill-cafés by the market.
Tuck into piri-piri chicken,
fries, salad and wine outside,
or under the awnings for live
soccer on TV. Around €12 for
a full meal.

Portimão, Praia da Rocha and around

Large and functional, Portimão is not particularly handsome, but it remains the best place to catch a boat trip up the coast, and its largely pedestrianized central streets make it one of the area's best places for shoppers. Virtually a suburb of Portimão, Praia da Rocha was one of the first Algarve tourist developments thanks to its enormous, broad sandy beach, framed by jagged rock formations and a clifftop fort, and it remains one of the region's most visited resorts. There are fine beaches to be enjoyed west of Portimão at Praia do Vau and Praia de Três Irmãos, which merges with Praia de Alvor, the best stretch of sand in the area. This peters out at the picturesque estuary of the Rio de Alvor, near the Quinta da Rocha seabird refuge. The town of Alvor itself is an erstwhile fishing village with a characterful riverfront harbour.

Portimão centre

Known as Portus Magnus in Roman times, Portimão became a major departure point for the great Portuguese explorers: Bartolomeu Dias set off from here in 1487 to become the first European to round the southern tip of Africa. The modern town of Portimão is dominated by pedestrianized shopping streets and graceless concrete high-rises

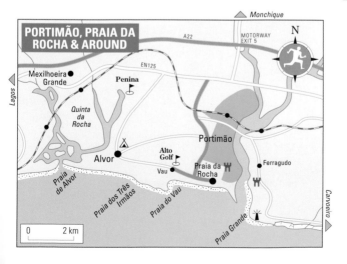

Visiting Portimão

The train station is inconveniently located at the northern tip of town on Largo Ferra Prado. From here a bus runs every 45 minutes (Mon–Fri) into the centre; a taxi costs about €5, or it's a fifteen-minute walk. Buses (including those to and from Praia da Rocha) pull up much more centrally, in the streets around the Largo do Duque, close to the river, where there are plenty of car-parking spots. The turismo is on Avenida Zeca Afonso, opposite the football stadium on the Praia da Rocha road (Mon–Sat 9.30am–5.30pm; ☎282 416 556).

– the majority of the older buildings were destroyed in the 1755 earthquake. The most historic building is the Igreja da Nossa Senhora da Conceição, rebuilt after the earthquake but retaining a Manueline door from the original fourteenth-century structure; the interior is more impressive, with three aisles and a vaulted ceiling. The walls are covered in seventeenth-century decorative *azulejos*.

The surrounding streets are pleasant enough, filled with shops catering to day-trippers

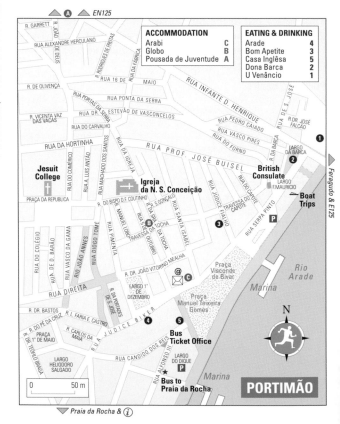

ACCOMMODATION

Arabi	C
Globo	B
Pousada de Juventude	A

EATING & DRINKING

Arade	4
Bom Apetite	3
Casa Inglêsa	5
Dona Barca	2
U Venâncio	1

PORTIMÃO

▲ AZULEJOS IN PORTIMÃO'S MAIN SQUARE

– selling lace, shoes, jewellery, ceramics and wicker goods; the main shopping streets are around the pedestrianized Rua Diogo Tomé and Rua da Portades de São José. Just off the latter lies Largo 1 de Dezembro, an atmospheric square with benches inlaid with *azulejos* depicting Portuguese historical scenes, including Pedro Álvares Cabral's landing in Brazil in 1500.

Portimão riverfront

The most attractive part of town is the riverfront gardens, a series of squares – Largo do Duque, Praça Manuel Teixeira Gomes and Praça Visconde de Bivar – with bustling cafés beneath shady trees right by the river. You'll be approached by people offering boat trips along the coast to see weird and wonderful grottoes, including trips to Carvoeiro, Lagos and even up the Rio Arade to Silves – all worthwhile trips.

Heading under the road bridge, you'll find a series of open-air restaurants serving grilled sardine lunches. The streets just back from the bridge – off Largo da Barca – are Portimão's oldest: narrow, cobbled and with more than a hint of their fishing-quarter past. Largo da Barca itself is a lovely little hidden square, lined with the tables of various upmarket fish restaurants (see p.139).

Praia da Rocha

Praia da Rocha ("beach of rock") is something of a misnomer as, despite the low cliffs and jagged rocks around it, the beach here is one of the deepest stretches of sand in the Algarve. Sadly, it is backed by rather characterless high-rise hotels, discos and a casino, though here and there among the hotel blocks fin-de-siècle villas testify to the resort's

Visiting Praia da Rocha

Bus connections from Portimão depart every fifteen to thirty minutes, leaving from the stop just south of Largo do Duque (daily 7.30am–11.30pm; €1.80 single). If you plan to do much toing and froing between Rocha and Portimão, buy a block of ten tickets from a kiosk in Portimão, and you'll save around fifty percent on the fare.

The turismo (daily: May–Sept 9.30am–7pm; Oct–April 9.30am–5.30pm; ☎282 419 132) is due to move to a new home by the Katedral disco by 2008.

more upmarket past. Most of the modern development is channelled into a strip just two blocks wide north of the main street, Avenida Tomás Cabreira; from the *avenida* steep steps lead down to the sands.

The west end of the beach is marked by a *miradouro* with further views up the coast, though this end of Avenida Tomás Cabreira is tackier and more commercialized than the eastern end.

▼ VAU BEACH

Fortaleza da Santa Caterina

The low walls of the Fortaleza da Santa Caterina cap the eastern end of the Avenida Tomás Cabreira. Built in 1691 to protect the mouth of the River Arade, the fort contains a small café and offers splendid views at sunset – beach and ocean on one side, Ferragudo, the marina and river on the other; there's also a small garden below the fort with great views back over the beach. Down the steep steps to the beach below the castle, you can walk out along the harbour walls for more fine views back to the fort.

Vau, Praia de Três Irmãos and Praia de Alvor

Regular daily buses run from Portimão to Alvor along the coastal stretch, calling at all the beaches en route. Vau is an undistinguished resort facing a lovely, typically Algarvian beach backed by rock pillars and cliffs. The town's apartments make up a fairly characterless settlement, but there are plenty of clifftop restaurants if you fancy stopping for a meal.

Separated by a rocky headland – which you can walk round

in twenty minutes or so – lies another fine stretch of sands, Praia de Três Irmãos, which becomes Praia de Alvor. Both beaches are backed by villas and hotels, but there's usually enough space to lay your towel with a little privacy, even in high season.

Alvor

Set on a river estuary a short walk from a splendid beach, Alvor is one of the Algarve's most characterful towns, though these days modern, low-rise buildings outnumber its Moorish core. Although much of the town was razed in the 1755 earthquake, it still boasts a sixteenth-century **Igreja Matriz** with superb Manueline doors, arches and pillars carved into fishing ropes and exotic plants. The area around the church and the central Praça da República is the most enjoyable and atmospheric part of town, and the harbour itself is a delight, lined with colourful fishing boats and fish restaurants.

You can still make out the vestiges of Alvor's thirteenth-century castle, now a leafy ruin containing a children's playground. Opposite the castle lies the small covered fruit and vegetable market, which usually gets going at 7am (Mon–Sat).

Alvor's liveliest street is Rua Dr. Frederico Romas Mendes, lined with bars and restaurants and culminating in a pedestrianized square, Largo da Ribeira, right on the

▲ ALVOR OLD TOWN

riverside. The square is marked by a quirky modern statue of a fish, appropriately marking the old fish market (now deserted) and has half a dozen excellent fish restaurants. You get wonderful views from here of the picturesque estuary of the Rio Alvor, swooped over by seagulls and lined with beached fishing boats. Head right from the square as you face the river and a walkway leads up the estuary for an attractive *passeio*; alternatively, head left and a ten-minute walk past cafés and the fishermen's huts takes you to the extensive sands of Praia de Alvor.

Quinta da Rocha nature area

The Quinta da Rocha nature area lies on a peninsula between the mouths of the rivers Alvor and Odiáxere, northwest of Alvor's huge beach. It is an extensive area of citrus and almond groves, copses, salt

Visiting Alvor

Regular buses (roughly hourly) run to Alvor from Portimão. There are plenty of car-parking spots along the riverfront or down by the beach. The turismo is in the centre of town at Rua Dr. Alfonso Costa 51 (Mon–Fri: May–Sept 9.30am–12.30pm & 2–6pm; Oct–April 9.30am–1.30pm & 2–5.30pm; ☎282 457 540).

Portimão, Praia da Rocha and around PLACES

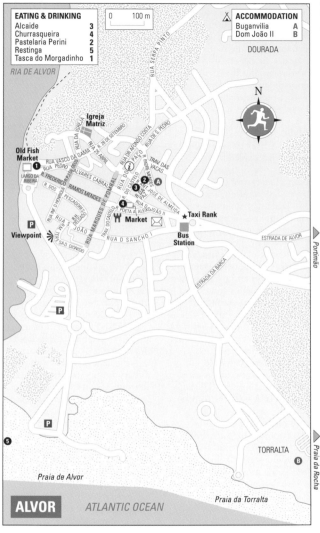

EATING & DRINKING
Alcaide	3
Churrasqueira	4
Pastelaria Perini	2
Restinga	5
Tasca do Morgadinho	1

ACCOMMODATION
Buganvilia	A
Dom João II	B

Penina & EN125

0   100 m

RIA DE ALVOR

DOURADA

N

Igreja Matriz

Old Fish Market

LARGO DA RIBEIRA

Viewpoint

Market

Taxi Rank

Bus Station

ESTRADA DE ALVOR

Portimão

Praia da Rocha

TORRALTA

Praia de Alvor

Praia da Torralta

ALVOR   ATLANTIC OCEAN

marshes, sandy spits and estuarine mud flats, all offering a wide range of habitats for different plants and animals – including 22 species of wading bird. Flanked by the Penina Golf Club to the northeast and the Palmares Golf Club to the west (see p.185), the area remains vulnerable, as protected status has not been secured, despite attempts by environmentalists; for the time being, however, development is being kept at bay.

With a car, the best approach to the reserve is along the

▲ QUINTA DA ROCHA

small turning off the EN125 opposite Mexilheira Grande, signed Benavides/Quinta da Rocha. Within the nature area there are plenty of narrow roads and tracks around the estuary where you can see wading birds and clam fishermen.

Accommodation

Hotel Bela Vista

Avda Tomás Cabreira, Praia da Rocha ☎282 450 480, ⓦwww.hotelbelavista .net. The most stylish place to stay on the seafront, this pseudo-Moorish mansion was built in 1903; the interior is an exquisite mixture of carved woods, stained glass, and yellow, white and blue *azulejos*. Rooms are large and airy – €5 extra gets you a balcony – and there's a great downstairs beach-facing terrace. €120.

Hospedaria Buganvilia

Rua Padre Mendes 6, Alvor ☎282 459 412. Just down the hill from the turismo, this modern guesthouse offers spotless en-suite rooms. There's also a roof terrace and a decent downstairs restaurant. Minimum one week's stay in high season. €55.

Casa Três Palmeiras

Apt. 84, Praia do Vau ☎282 401 275, ⓦwww.casatrespalmeiras.com. Closed Dec & Jan. In an idyllic position on a clifftop above a little beach, this sleek villa is a superb example of 1960s design chic. Its glass-fronted rooms curve round a terrace with its own pool where breakfast is served in summer. Rooms and communal areas are spacious and tastefully furnished in traditional Portuguese style. Services include manicures, reflexology and massages on request, and discounts are available for local golf courses. €185.

Dom João II

Praia de Alvor ☎282 400 700, ⓦwww .pestana.com. Around 1km from Alvor, facing the beach, this is the most appealing of a row of high-rise hotels on this stretch. There's a large pool, kids' club, gym, sauna and restaurant, and guests have discounts at the nearby Tennis Country Club and the Pinta and Gramacha Golf Courses. In low season, prices are reduced by up to fifty percent. Disabled access. €210.

Hotel Globo

Rua 5 de Outubro 151, Portimão ☎282 416 350, ⓦhotelglobo.net. A good-value modern high-rise close to the Igreja Matriz. The decor is dull, but it has its own restaurant and upper rooms overlook the harbour. €105.

Hotel Jupiter

Avda Tomás Cabreira, Praia da Rocha ☎282 415 041, ⓦhoteljupiter.com. A modern hulk on the wrong (land) side of the *avenida*, but with comfortable rooms, gym and sauna plus disabled access. You pay €20 extra for sea views. There's also a bar, restaurant and small outdoor pool. €120.

Hotel Santa Catarina
Rua António Feu, Praia da Rocha ☎282 405 040, ⓦftphotels.com. Recently renovated, this plush hotel near the casino boasts fine views from the upper rooms (€20 extra), plus it has its own bar and restaurant. Not characterful but good value. €110.

Residencial Vila Lido
Avda Tomás Cabreira, Praia da Rocha ☎282 424 127, ☎282 424 246. Closed Nov–Feb. This beautiful blue-shuttered building with original, traditional Portuguese decor sits at the less tacky east end of the *avenida* in its own small grounds facing the fort; front rooms (€10 extra) have superb views over the beach. Evening meals on request. €105.

Youth hostel
Lugar do Coca, Maravilhas, Portimão ☎282 491 804, ⓦpousadasdejuventude.pt. A well-equipped, large, modern hostel with its own small swimming pool, bar, canteen, and sports facilities, including snooker and tennis courts. There are 49 double rooms, eight en suite. Currently being renovated; check the website for prices.

Campsite

Parque de Campismo Dourado
Estrada Monte de Alvor, Alvor ☎282 459 178, ⓦwww.roteiro-campista.pt. Around 1km north of Alvor, this is a pleasant, leafy campsite with decent facilities.

Cafés

Casa Inglêsa
Praça Manuel Teixeira Gomes, Portimão. Daily 8am–11pm. A large, cavernous café on the riverfront square, offering a good range of fresh juices and snacks; its sunny terrace is a popular meeting spot.

Pastelaria Arade
Largo 1º de Dezembro 4, Portimão. Daily 8.30am–9pm. A small, traditional *pastelaria* specializing in sweets and cakes from the Algarve, mostly almond-based marzipan.

Pastelaria Perini
Rua Dr. António José D'Almeida 4, Alvor. Daily 8am–midnight. Just downhill from the tourist office, this traditional *pastelaria* has a counter full of speciality home-made cakes; it also offers a good range of croissants and snacks such as crepes and pizzas.

Restaurants

O Alcaide
Rua do Castelo, Alvor ☎282 459 330. Daily noon–3pm & 7.30–11pm. A homely and intimate restaurant near Alvor's castle, with moderately priced grills and great *cataplanas* (fish stews).

Bom Apetite
Rua Júdice Fialho 21, Portimão. Mon–Sat 10.30am–2am. Bargain meat and fish dishes, including specialities from the Alentejo district such as *açorda de bacaulhau* and *migas* – both variants of garlicky bread sauce. The graffitoed bar area is also lively.

Churrasqueira

Mercado de Alvor, Alvor ☎282 458 248. Mon & Wed–Sun noon–3pm & 7.30–10pm. Classic Portuguese takeaway food, with a few sitdown tables on one corner of the market building. Superb-value chicken from €5.

Cervejaria Praia da Rocha

Edifício Colunas, Praia da Rocha ☎282 416 541. Daily noon–3pm & 7–11pm. Tucked away in a side street opposite the casino, this bustling *cervajaria* attracts a largely local clientele thanks to good-value daily specials and well-prepared fish and grills. Around €15 for a full meal.

Dona Barca

Largo da Barca, Portimão ☎282 484 189. Daily noon–3pm & 6–10pm. A very highly rated, expensive fish restaurant – it has frequently represented the Algarve at Lisbon's gastronomy fair – with an atmospheric interior and outdoor tables on this pretty square. It serves typical Algarve cuisine including *feijoada de Buzinas* (shellfish with beans) and regional desserts such as *tarte de amendoa* (almond tart).

La Dolce Vita

Avda Tomás Cabreira, Edifício Mar Azul, Praia da Rocha ☎282 419 444. Daily 11am–3pm & 6.30–10.30pm. A lively, inexpensive little place with rustic decor. It is owned and run by Italians, so the home-made pasta, pizzas, salads and ice creams are reliably tasty; set lunches start at €8 and there's live music at weekends.

Mar e Sol

Praia, Praia da Rocha ☎282 437 722. Mon & Wed–Sun 10am–10pm. Best value of the row of beachfront restaurants – each under a crab-like carapace of steel girders. The usual fish and grills come with a free beachside view. Full meals around €15.

Tasca do Margadinho

Largo da Ribeirinho 9, Alvor ☎282 459 144. Mon–Wed & Fri–Sun 10am–midnight. An atmospheric *tasca* (tavern) opposite the old fish market, moderately priced, with a local feel and superbly

▲ PORTIMÃO

grilled fresh fish; there are tables outside on the square, too.

A Portuguesa

Avda Tomás Cabreira, Praia da Rocha ☎282 424 175. Mon–Sat 3pm–1am. A welcoming restaurant specializing in substantial mid-priced Portuguese grills, backed by gentle jazzy sounds most nights. There are also pasta dishes and a few vegetarian options.

Restinga

Praia de Alvor ☎282 459 434. Daily 9am–9pm. Closed one month in winter. Sitting on the cusp of a large dune, this bar-restaurant offers stunning views of the beach and estuary, along with decent fish meals at moderate prices.

Safari

Rua António Feu, Praia da Rocha ☎282 423 540. Daily noon–10pm. This swish restaurant with attentive service overlooks the beach and serves mainly Portuguese dishes, a few with an international twist. The lamb stew and chicken curry are recommended. Mains from €9.

U Venâncio

Zona Ribeirinha Entre-Pontes 4, Portimão ☎963 456 901. Daily 11am–midnight. The best of the row of smart but inexpensive fish restaurants facing the river, specializing in grilled sardines, though other fish and meat also feature.

Bars and clubs

Katedral

Avda Tomás Cabreira, Praia da Rocha. ⓦwww.katedraldisco.com. June–Sept daily midnight–6am; Oct–May Thurs–Sat midnight–6am. Housed in a futuristic cube-shaped building on the clifftop, this is the largest and highest-profile club in town, with a lightshow and the latest dance sounds. The downstairs bar, *Nicho*, is a good place to start the evening.

Moonlight Bar

Rua António Feu, Praia da Rocha. Daily 9pm–4am. Bright decor, lively sounds and a superb terrace facing the beach where you can while the night away.

On the Rocks

Avda Tomás Cabreira, Lojas B & C, Praia da Rocha ☎282 416 144, ⓦwww.discobarontherocks.com. Daily 10am–4am. A modern dance bar with a sunny terrace where you can catch the sunset before loud music takes hold inside. Live soccer on TV sometimes vies for attention in the bar; there's also a dance floor and live music on Fridays.

Pé de Vento

Avda Tomás Cabreira Loja A, Praia da Rocha ☎282 424 180. Daily 3pm–4am. Another popular disco bar over two floors. The upstairs bar has a beach-facing terrace next to a large dance floor that features live music on Wednesdays.

Serra de Monchique

Forming the natural northern boundary to the Algarve, the Serra de Monchique is a delightful green and wooded mountain range of cork, chestnut and eucalyptus trees. Though frequently damaged by summer fires, the woodland is usually quick to recover and it remains ideal hiking country, embracing the region's highest peak at Fóia, located near the area's main town, Monchique. It also has one of the country's most picturesque spa resorts, Caldas de Monchique, and a small theme park.

Monchique

Monchique is a small hill town whose large market on the second Monday of each month is famous for smoked hams and locally made furniture – especially distinctive X-shaped wooden chairs. You'll see more local produce every Sunday in the modern main square, whose salient feature is a fountain that feeds a traditional *nora*, or well. Uphill from here, the old town, dotted with beautifully crafted metal sculptures of local characters made by the contemporary Lisbon artist Doutor Vanancio,

▲ NOSSA SONHORA DO DESTERRO

is a fine place for a wander. The most impressive building is the parish church, the Igreja Matriz (Mon–Sat 10am–5.30pm), up a steep cobbled street from the main square, with an imposing Manueline porch and, inside, a little chapel covered with *azulejos*.

SERRA DE MONCHIQUE

Visiting Monchique

Buses from Portimão arrive at the terminal in the main square, Largo 5 de Outubro. Head uphill on the Fóia road and 200m on, by a large modern viewpoint, you'll find Monchique's helpful turismo (May–Sept Mon–Fri 9.30am–12.30pm & 2–6pm; Oct–April Mon–Fri 9.30am–1pm & 2–5.30pm; ☎282 911 189) alongside an underground car park.

The most evocative of the town's sights, though, is the ruined seventeenth-century Franciscan monastery of **Nossa Senhora do Desterro**, of which only a roofless shell survives, and even that looks close to collapse. To get here follow signs through the old town and along a wooded track past giant cork trees and chestnut woods – a lovely fifteen-minute walk.

Fóia

No public transport. The 900-metre peak of Fóia is the highest in the Serra de Monchique. It's a lovely journey to the summit, winding up wooded slopes dotted with upmarket inns (see pp.143–144) and *miradouros* offering far-reaching views over the south coast. Bristling with antennae and radio masts and capped by an ungainly modern complex of a café-restaurant and shop, the summit itself can be an anticlimax, especially if clouds obscure the views or you have to share the experience with multitudes in midsummer. Get here before 10am if you can. On a clear day the panoramic view from the top takes in Portimão, Lagos, the foothills stretching to the Barragem da Bravura, and Cabo de São Vicente in the west.

Caldas de Monchique

Caldas de Monchique, set in a steep valley and surrounded by thick woods, has been a spa since Roman times. It is particularly spectacular in autumn when the deciduous trees – a relative rarity in Portugal – display fantastic colours. In the nineteenth century the town became a favourite resort for the Spanish bourgeoisie, though these days it's coach parties that fill its main square, in high season at least. The waters are still said to have healing powers for skin and chest complaints. In recent

▼ VIEW FROM FÓIA

▲ MANSION, CALDAS DE MONCHIQUE

years the whole place has been revitalized and turned into a tourist resort; old buildings have been sympathetically restored.

Halfway down the hill on the left you'll see the cobbled, tree-shaded main square, fronted by the pseudo-Moorish windows of the former casino – now an exhibition centre – and flanked by lovely, nineteenth-century buildings. Downhill from the main square you pass the Bouvet – a little stone building where you can drink the therapeutic waters free, straight from the ground. Heading uphill, you can follow the stream out of the village to a tranquil picnic spot shaded by giant eucalyptus trees.

Caldas de Monchique spa

☎282 910 910, ⓦwww .monchiquetermas.com. Mon 9am–1pm, Tues 10.30am–1pm & 3–7pm, Wed–Sun 9–1pm & 3–7pm. €25. Caldas de Monchique's cutting-edge thermal spa lies downhill from the main square and offers various specialist water treatments on the ground floor of a modern hotel. The entrance fee gives access to the sauna, steam room, gym, water massage facilities and pool, with extra sessions ranging from a thirty-minute "chocolate face mask" treatment (€90) to full body massages from €55. Discounts of twenty percent are available to hotel guests.

Parque da Mina

Sítio do Vale de Boi ☎282 911 622, ⓦwww.parquedamina.pt. Daily: April–Sept 10am–7pm; Oct–March 10am–5pm. €8, children €5. Set on partly wooded and partly open land on the site of a deactivated mine, this theme park offers diverse attractions for all ages. For younger kids there's a mini farm, woodland walks and picnic areas, while older children can take part in various adventure sports. The highlight is a visit to a gallery of the old copper, quartz and iron mine which was operational until the 1960s, and an eighteenth-century house containing a re-created *medronho* distillery. Adventure sports (some of which incur additional fees) include paintballing, trip-wire rides and a climbing wall.

Accommodation

Abrigo da Montanha

Estrada da Fóia ☎282 912 131, ⓦabrigodamontanha.com. Just out of Monchique on the Fóia road, this modern granite-and-wood chalet-style inn has comfortable rooms with great views over the valley. There's also a pool, a downstairs restaurant, and a roaring fire when the air turns chilly. €80.

Visiting Caldas de Monchique

Regular buses from Portimão pass the turning to Caldas on their way to and from Monchique. Some of these call into the centre of Caldas, though most stop instead on the main road five minutes out of town.

▲ MONCHIQUE BACKSTREETS

Albergaria do Lageado

Caldas de Monchique ☎282 912 616,
📠282 911 310. Closed Nov–April.
Just above the main square, this
characterful four-star hotel has
twenty smart rooms, with TVs
and en-suite bathrooms. There's
a pool in the garden and an
excellent restaurant. €55.

Hotel Central

Caldas de Monchique ☎282 910
910, ⓦwww.monchiquetermas.com.
A very comfortable three-star
partly set in the former casino
building; modern comforts
include fridges, satellite TV and
a/c. €130.

Dom Francisco

Caldas de Monchique ☎282 910 910,
ⓦwww.monchiquetermas.com. The
spa parent company hires out
neat apartments overlooking the
main square, with small living
rooms and kitchenettes, sleeping
up to four people from €160
a night.

Estrela de Monchique

Rua do Porto Fundo 46, Monchique
☎282 913 111. Just to the east of
the bus terminal, this is much

the best budget option in town,
with bright, modern en-suite
rooms; top-floor rooms have
balconies. The price does not
include breakfast. €40.

Quinta de São Bento

Estrada da Fóia ☎282 912 700,
ⓦwww.quintasaobento.online
.pt. Around 1km below the
Fóia summit, this wonderful
old stone *quinta* is set on
a peaceful slope amongst
chestnut woods. Owned by
members of the Bragança family
– former monarchs of Portugal
– it is full of antiques, with five
comfortable rooms and one
apartment. It is also famed for
its cuisine (see opposite). €70.

Shops

Loja do Chocolate

Rua do Porto Fundo 16, Monchique.
Daily 9am–8pm. A cornucopia
of sweets and chocolates, run
by a British family. The home-
made chocolates – including
chocolate-coated fruits, such
as strawberries – can be kept
unrefrigerated and make good
gifts to take home.

Cafés and bars

A Casa da Nora

Largo 25 de Outubro, Monchique.
Daily 9am–9pm. Named after the
traditional well that still operates
opposite, this bustling café-bar
next to the turismo offers good-
value snacks and light meals.
Tables spill onto the attractive
main square.

Barlefante

Travessa dos Guerreiras, Monchique.
Sun–Thurs noon–1am, Fri & Sat
1pm–4am. A fashionable café-bar
consisting of a series of cave-like

rooms with a few outdoor tables on a quiet side alley. Snacks, shots and cocktails, with good sounds.

O Tasco

Caldas de Monchique. Daily 9am–8pm. On the far side of the main square, below the path to the picnic area, this darkened bar is housed in the oldest building in the village, in sixteenth-century stables. Specialities include bread rolls with sausagemeat baked in a traditional oven outside.

Restaurants

Restaurante 1692

Caldas de Monchique ☎282 910 910. Daily 10am–8pm. A high-profile, formal and expensive restaurant named after its year of construction, with lovely outdoor tables under the trees of the main square. The menu includes interesting starters such as *morcelo* (spicy sausage), followed by conventional grilled fish and meat dishes.

Restaurante Central

Rua da Igreja 5, Monchique ☎282 913 160. Daily 11am–7.30pm. A tiny place smothered with notes and postcards detailing past visitors' comments – mainly complimentary. The menu is limited to two or three average Portuguese dishes, but the place scores high on character, and dishes are inexpensive.

Restaurante A Charrete

Rua Dr. Samora Gil 30–34, Monchique ☎282 912 142. Mon–Wed & Fri–Sun 12.30–10pm. This smart restaurant on the road up to the convent is the best place to eat in Monchique, specializing in award-winning but not too pricey "mountain food" – cooked with beans, pasta

and rice – along with more conventional Algarve fare. Desserts include a superb *pudim de mel* (honey pudding). Around €25 for a full meal.

Restaurante Quinta de São Bento

Estrada da Fóia ☎282 912 143. Tues–Sun noon–3pm & 7–10pm. It's worth booking ahead for a meal at this superb *quinta* (see opposite) just below Fóia. The award-winning cuisine features regional specialities, prepared with local produce such as Monchique ham, goat's cheese, *chouriço*, almonds and figs. Pricey but worth it.

O Rouxinol

Caldas de Monchique ☎282 913 975. Tues–Sun noon–10pm. Closed Dec & Jan. A highly rated restaurant set in a former hunting lodge on the main road just above town. With a giant fireplace – large enough to roast a whole pig – the inside is very cosy but there's also an outdoor terrace facing wooded slopes. The Swedish owners serve Portuguese and international dishes, salads and great desserts. Around €25 for a full meal.

▼ STREET STATUE, MONCHIQUE

Lagos and around

At the mouth of the Rio Bensafrim, its historic centre enclosed in largely fourteenth-century town walls, lies Lagos, one of the Algarve's most attractive and historic towns. In 1577, Lagos became the administrative capital of the Algarve, and continued to flourish until much of the town was destroyed in the 1755 earthquake. Today it's a thriving resort, but it also remains a working fishing port and market centre with a life of its own. Lagos's main attraction is its proximity to some of the best beaches on the Algarve coast. To the east of the town is a long sweep of sand – Meia Praia – while to the west lies an extraordinary network of cove beaches, including Praia de Dona Ana, Praia do Pinhão and Praia do Camilo, accessible in summer on a toy train. Two different attractions lie a short drive inland: a beautiful reservoir, the Barragem de Bravura, and Lagos Zoo, a good outing for families.

Avenida dos Descobrimentos

The palm-lined Avenida dos Descobrimentos hugs the banks of the river and offers some of the best views of Lagos's old town walls. At the *avenida*'s western end, the squat seventeenth-century **Forte da Ponta da Bandeira** (Tues–Sun 9.30am–12.30pm & 2–5pm; €2.05) guards the entrance to the harbour. The fort itself is rather uninteresting, its interior consisting of a small temporary exhibition space, though you can enjoy fine views over the water from its ramparts. Lagos's **mercado**, the bustling fruit, vegetable and fish market, also lies on the *avenida*. A rambling Saturday market can also be found around the bus station.

Most days, stalls set up along the *avenida*'s length offering boat trips to the surrounding coastline (see box p.151), with many trips departing from the smart marina.

LAGOS & AROUND

The marina

Backed by shops and international restaurants and filled with flash yachts, the marina is reached by a swing bridge over the river. You can

▲ LAGOS RIVERFRONT

continue beyond it to Meia
Praia (see p.150) via Lagos's
characterful fishing harbour.
The marina also marks the
starting point of the **toy train**
(May–Sept hourly 10am–11pm;
€3), which trundles along
Avenida dos Descobrimentos
and out via the beaches of
Praia Dona Ana and Porto de

Visiting Lagos

Lagos is the western terminal of the
Algarve rail line and its train station
is fifteen minutes' walk from the
town centre. The bus station (☎282
762 944) is a block back from the
main Avenida dos Descobrimentos.
There is free parking around the
bridge to the marina on Avenida dos
Descobrimentos, though you need
to pay to park in the other spaces
around the old town.

The turismo (daily: May–Sept
9.30am–7pm; Oct–April 9.30am–
5.30pm; ☎282 763 031) is at Sítio
de São João, which is the first
roundabout as you come into the
town from the east. From the centre, it's a twenty-minute walk; keep
going down Rua Vasco da Gama,
past the bus station.

Moz to the headland at Ponta
da Piedade. The trip takes
around 25 minutes one-way.

The slave market and Praça da República

In one corner of the leafy Praça
da República, under the arcades
of the old Customs House,
you'll find a diminutive unsigned
space that was Europe's first
slave market (*mercado de escravos*).
The market opened in 1444,
and within a hundred years up
to 10,000 slaves were being
shipped from Africa annually to
meet Portuguese demand alone.
Nowadays the Customs House
serves as an art gallery, showing
local art.

Opposite the old slave market
sits the church of **Santa Maria**.
The young king of Portugal,
Dom Sebastião, is said to have
roused his troops in front of
the church before the ill-fated
Moroccan expedition of 1578,
from which the king never
returned.

Praça Luís de Camões and Praça Gil Eanes

From Praça da República,
the narrow streets of the old

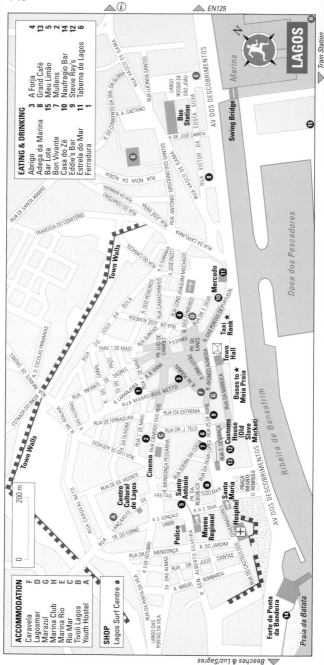

▲ LAGOS OLD TOWN

town straggle east to two other attractive mosaic-paved and pedestrianized squares, Praça Luís de Camões and Praça Gil Eanes, around which you'll find Lagos's best cafés, restaurants and guesthouses. The latter square is fronted by Lagos's grand-looking Neoclassical town hall, but its most prominent feature is a peculiar modern statue of an adolescent Dom Sebastião, resembling a flowerpot man.

Museu Regional and Igreja de Santo António

Rua General, Alberto Silveira. Tues–Sun 9.30am–12.30pm & 2–5pm. €2.05. The Museu Regional shoehorns in just about every possible historical and quirky object relating to Lagos and the Algarve, and the random nature of the displays is all part of the appeal.

The most important items are visible on either side as you enter, including Roman remains from the dig at Boca do Rio (see p.158), featuring an amphora encrusted with coral and busts of Roman emperor Galiano, as well as an impressive wall-mounted decorative mosaic. Elsewhere, there are Neolithic axeheads, Visigothic stone coffins, jars containing misshapen animal foetuses, a display of models of Algarvian chimneys, stuffed goats, straw hats and basketry, model fishing boats, travelogues and the 1504 town charter; there are also collections of coins, medals and banknotes, sacred art, weaponry and some frightening early surgical instruments.

The Portuguese expeditions

Lagos played an important role in setting the Portuguese maritime explorations in motion. Gil Eanes, the first explorer to round Cape Bojador, was born in Lagos and set sail from here in 1434. Also in the fifteenth century, Henry the Navigator used the port of Lagos as a base for the new African trade. These early voyages paved the way for even greater explorations, which eventually enabled Portugal to become one of the richest countries in the world, with an empire stretching from Brazil in the west to Macau in the east.

▲ FALLING FROM THE CLIFF-BACKED COVE BEACHES

You exit the museum through the extraordinary interior of the neighbouring Igreja de Santo António. It was decorated in around 1715, and every inch of the nave is exuberantly carved, right up to and including the barrel-vaulted ceiling – representing the life of Santo António.

Meia Praia

Served by regular bus from Avenida dos Descobrimentos, or a 30min walk over the footbridge via the marina and fishing harbour. Opposite Lagos, east of the river, Meia Praia is a stunning tract of soft sand stretching 4km to the delta of the rivers Odiáxere and Arão. Flanked by the railway line and set well back from the road, the wide beach gets progressively quieter the further you get away from town towards the greenery of the Palmares Golf Club. The beach is particularly popular with backpackers, and there are plenty of beachside cafés and restaurants along this stretch of coastline.

Praia da Batata

Despite being right on the edge of town, just beyond the Forte Ponta da Bandeira, Praia da Batata (Potato Beach) is an alluring stretch of sand, reached through a natural rock tunnel. In late August, the town beach is the venue for the Banho festival, an annual beach party marking the end of summer, with evening barbecues, live music and a traditional midnight swim.

Praia do Pinhão

Praia do Pinhão, a lovely, sheltered, sandy bay beneath steep cliffs, is the first of the cove beaches tucked into the promontory south of Lagos. It is around fifteen minutes' walk from Lagos – follow Avenida dos Descobrimentos up the hill (towards Sagres) and it's signed left just opposite the fire station.

Praia de Dona Ana

Praia de Dona Ana is one of the most photogenic of all the Algarve's beaches, a wide expanse of sand framed by cliffs, weirdly sculpted rock pillars and caves. In high season the sands are heaving; and the cliffs above it are lined with cafés, hotels and apartments. You can walk here along the clifftop path from Praia do Pinhão; the beach can also be reached from Lagos on the seasonal toy train (see p.147).

Praia do Camilo

Reached by a dramatically steep set of steps down a cliff, Praia do Camilo is another fine beach backed by natural rock art. A tunnel has been cut to link its two coves, with a fantastic natural cave – accessible from the sea – hidden in the rocks between the two. The beach is well signed off the coast road and can also be reached by the toy train (see p.147).

Ponta da Piedade

Tall palms and a handsome lighthouse mark the craggy headland of Ponta da Piedade, a great vantage point for the sunset. It has sweeping views down the coast and a handy café. This is also the final port of call for the toy train from Lagos (see p.147). Steep steps descend the cliff to the east of the headland to a tiny bay where fishermen offer boat trips to the neighbouring grottoes (see box on below).

Porto de Mós

A fine sweep of golden sands backed by rugged cliffs forms Porto de Mós, the largest of the cove beaches west of Lagos. The approach to the beach is fairly developed, with a smattering of restaurants, but the sands are extensive enough to absorb the crowds.

A popular coastal path starts above the beach, climbing over the hills to Luz (see p.156), an exhilarating hour's walk away.

Barragem de Bravura

The Barragem de Bravura is one of the most picturesque of the Algarve's several *barragens* (reservoirs), plugged by a huge dam over the River Bravura. To the south of the dam, the deep valley is little more than

▲ LIGHTHOUSE AT PONTA DA PIEDADE

an overgrown stream fed by a waterfall from the dam, while behind the dam lie the deep, still green waters of the reservoir, stirred by basking carp. It's an idyllic spot, and you can walk right over the top of the dam and round the edges of the reservoir on the other side along a dirt trail. Swimming, fishing and watersports, however, are prohibited.

There is no public transport to the Barragem de Bravura, but with your own transport it is a lovely seventeen-kilometre drive from Lagos through unspoilt countryside.

Boat trips and dolphin-watching

Because of its position and the diversity of trips on offer, Lagos is a great place to get a boat to see the surrounding coastline. Most trips cost around €10 per person for a 45-minute trip, up to €30 or so for half-day sailing rides or dolphin "seafaris". The best trip is to the coastline off Ponta da Piedade (see opposite), an amazing sculpture park of pillars, caves and rock arches – take a small fishing boat and you'll go right inside some of the caves. Dolphin-watching can also be unforgettable if you find a pod of playful common dolphins (and very occasionally whales or turtles), though to find them the high-powered boats sometimes have to cover huge distances at hair-raising speeds. "Guaranteed" sightings may actually mean a free ride on the next day's boat if you fail to find any.

Lagos Zoo

Quinta Figueiros, Barão de São João ⓦ www.zoolagos.com. Daily: April–Sept 10am–7pm; Oct–March 10am–5pm. €8, children €5, family ticket €21. Set in thirty square kilometres of semi-tropical parkland, this well-tended zoo is a great destination for families and is keen to publicize its environmental awareness. There are various birds including flamingos, toucans, owls, parrots and emus, as well as smaller mammals such as wallabies and porcupines. A "monkey lake" has various gibbons and smaller monkeys wandering semi-free on an island. There are also farm animals in a special children's enclosure that children can help feed at certain times. A shop, decent restaurants and children's playgrounds help break up the day.

Accommodation

Pensão Caravela

Rua 25 de Abril 8, Lagos ⓣ 282 763 361, ⓔ pensaocaravela@netvisao.pt. In a great position right on the old town's main pedestrianized street, the rooms here are clean though pretty basic. Doubles come with or without bath. €37.

Pensão Lagosmar

Rua Dr. Faria e Silva 13, Lagos ⓣ 282 763 523, ⓦ dfhoteis.com. An upmarket *pensão*, with spotless rooms mostly facing a quiet side street. All rooms have TVs and private bathrooms while some also have little balconies. There's also a small bar. €75.

Residencial Marazul

Rua 25 de Abril 13, Lagos ⓣ 282 770 230, ⓦ pensaomarazul.com. Closed Oct–March. A beautifully decorated *residencial*, with bright rooms and communal areas tiled in *azulejos*. En-suite bedrooms vary in size, but all come with TVs and some have terraces with sea views. €40.

Marina Club

Marina de Lagos, Lagos ⓣ 282 790 600, ⓦ www.marinaclub.pt. Avoid the front rooms overlooking a scrubby car park and go for one of the bright, minimalist modern rooms or spacious apartments facing the marina or the hotel's large swimming pool and terrace. The sleek decor is complemented by swish spa facilities. €110.

Albergaria Marina Rio

Avda dos Descobrimentos 388, Lagos ⓣ 282 769 859, ⓦ www.marinario .com. An ungainly, large modern inn offering decent rooms plus satellite TV, a games room and a rooftop pool. Front rooms face the harbour across the busy *avenida* (back rooms face the bus station). €101.

Meia Praia Beach Club

Meia Praia ⓣ 282 789 400, ⓦ www .dompedro.com. Around ten minutes' drive out of Lagos, just back from one of the best stretches of beach, this tasteful three-star is set in attractive grounds; the best rooms have sea-facing balconies. Apartments for 4–6 people are also on offer. There are tennis courts, a pool, and guests are entitled to discounts at the Palmares Golf Course (see p.185). €130.

Hotel Rio Mar

Rua Cândido dos Reis 83, Lagos ⓣ 282 763 091, ⓔ riomar@clix.pt. A smart, pleasantly old-fashioned hotel with its own bar, on a central street. Most rooms have a balcony – the best overlook the sea at the back of the hotel, others overlook a fairly quiet main street. €60.

Tivoli Lagos

Rua Antonío C. dos Santos, Lagos ☎ 282 790 079, ⊛ www.tivolilagos .com. Lagos's most upmarket central hotel is built round a central garden area with its own pool. Not all the rooms are spacious and some overlook a busy street, but the best have terraces with fine views over town. Two restaurants, indoor and outdoor pools and a health club plus a courtesy bus to its own beach club at Meia Praia make up its four-star appeal. €170.

Youth hostel

Rua de Lançarote de Freitas 50, Lagos ☎ 282 761 970, ⓔ lagos@movijovem .pt. Set around a central courtyard, this modern, well-designed youth hostel, just up from the Centro Cultural de Lagos, has several four-bed dorms (€16) plus a few en-suite doubles (€45); be sure to book in advance. There's Internet access and currency exchange.

Campsite

Parque de Campismo da Trindade

Rossio da Trindade ☎ 282 763 893, ⓕ 282 762 885. A basic, cramped campsite with a small shop, on the way to Praia de Dona Ana. In season, a bus marked "D. Ana/Porto de Mós" runs to the site from the bus station. On foot, it's about ten to fifteen minutes from the Forte Ponta da Bandeira. A taxi from the centre costs around €7.

Shops

Lagos Surf Centre

Rua Silva Lopes 31, Lagos. Mon–Sat 9.30am–8pm. A fashionable shop with a fine array of reasonably priced surfy clothes: shirts, shorts, T-shirts and trainers as well as surf gear. It can also arrange surf lessons.

Cafés

Cervejaria Abrigo

Rua Marquês de Pombal 2, Lagos. Mon–Sat 8.30am–9.30pm. With outdoor tables on a little square under scented orange trees, this aromatic café makes a great breakfast stop, with fluffy fresh croissants; it also serves beer, cocktails, snacks and meals all day.

Gaivota Branca

Meia Praia. Daily 10am–midnight. The perfect beachside café, set just over the railway lines on an idyllic stretch of beach opposite the *Dom Pedro Hotel*, the "white seagull" serves the usual range of snacks and seafood as well as drinks.

Naufragio

Avda dos Descobrimentos, Lagos. Daily 10am–2am. A pleasant

▼ A CAFÉ IN LAGOS OLD TOWN

beach café-bar with a youthful clientele, jazzy sounds and moderately priced bar snacks. Out the back there's a great terrace facing the town beach and the Forte da Ponta da Bandeira.

Restaurants

Adega da Marina

Avda dos Descobrimentos 35, Lagos ☎282 764 284. Daily noon–2am. Set in a former warehouse, this great barn of a place serves excellent food at tables lined up as if for a wedding party. It does huge portions of charcoal-grilled meat and fish plus great house wines and very good-value set meals for around €10.

António

Praia Porto de Mós ☎282 763 560. Daily 10am–10pm. Occupying a prime position, with a terrace facing the beach at Porto de Mós, *António* serves good food at reasonable prices. Great salads, fresh fish and grills from around €8, along with a range of pizzas and snacks.

Bar Lota

Doca Pesca, Lagos ☎282 764 048. Daily noon–10pm. At the station end of the fishing harbour, this is very much a local haunt with wooden benches as rough-looking as the clientele – but the fresh fish, as you'd expect, is hard to beat. Tables inside and out.

Casa do Zé

Avda dos Descobrimentos, Lagos. Daily 6am–2am. A tiny bar-restaurant next to the market, with outside seats facing the harbour offering filling dishes – mostly fish but some meat – from an inexpensive menu chalked up on the board.

Estrela do Mar

Mercado Municipal, Lagos ☎282 769 250. Tues–Sat noon–3pm & 7–10pm, Sun noon–3pm. Atop the main market building and boasting fine views from its terrace, this swish place serves fresh fish straight from the market, along with its speciality, *cataplana* stews. It's not cheap (around €20 for a full meal), but live music on alternate Saturdays adds to the attraction.

A Forja

Rua dos Ferreiros 17, Lagos ☎282 768 588. Mon–Fri & Sun noon–3pm & 7–11pm. Despite a rather bland interior, *A Forja* is usually full by 8pm thanks to very good-value and tasty fresh fish (from around €8). It also serves a few grilled meat dishes, omelettes and tasty starters.

Meu Limão

Rua Silva Lopes 40–42, Lagos ☎282 767 946. Daily 11am–11pm. A very popular tapas bar-restaurant with a pleasant tiled interior and a few outdoor tables. Fresh and tangy tapas from €3–6 are available, plus some unusual mains including chicken with mango, vegetarian burgers and Mexican steak with chilli.

Mirante

Praia de Dona Ana. Daily 9am–midnight. Right on the cliff overlooking the sands, this is a great place to enjoy the house specialities such as *espetada de tamboril* (monkfish kebab) and *norvilho na brasa* (char-grilled steaks). It also does moderately priced snacks and a range of drinks.

Taberna de Lagos

Rua 25 de Abril, Lagos ☎282 084 250. Daily 6pm–1am. A lovely, high-ceilinged eighteenth-century mansion converted into a sophisticated bar-restaurant that attracts an arty crowd. Pricey but tasty food includes steaks, kebabs, fresh fish (mains from around €15) and less expensive tapas and salads. Also does a fine range of cocktails.

Bars and clubs

Bon Vivante

Rua 25 Abril 105, Lagos. Daily 6pm–4am. Just north of the old slave market, this late-night disco bar has gaudy marble pillars and a superb "tropical" roof terrace that catches the last of the day's sun; a good place to hit when the other bars have closed.

Eddie's Bar

Rua 25 de Abril 99, Lagos ☎282 768 329. Daily 4pm–2am. A small, dark-wood bar with a good selection of sounds and attracting a friendly crowd. Live soccer and sports are often shown on a screen at the back.

Cervejaria Ferradura

Rua 1° de Maio 26a, Lagos. Mon–Sat 10am–2am. An atmospheric *cervajaria* – very much a locals'

place – with walls covered in soccer posters and stacks of inexpensive *petiscos* on the bar.

Grand Café

Rua Senhora da Graça 7, Lagos. April–Sept daily 9pm–4am; Oct–March Fri & Sat 9pm–4am. A superb high-ceilinged building decked in gold leaf and velvet, and one of the town's coolest hang-outs. There's an outside terrace, guest DJs and lively sounds.

Mullens

Rua Cândido dos Reis 86, Lagos ☎282 761 281. Daily 8pm–2am. This atmospheric, cavernous *adega* is the most appealing late-night choice in town. Inexpensive drinks including Guinness, sangria and *vinho verde* on tap are served alongside excellent and moderately priced meals to a jazz and soul soundtrack.

Stevie Ray's

Rua Senhora da Graça 9, Lagos ⓦwww.stevierays.com. Mon–Sat 9pm–4am. Lagos's premier jazz club, with live music every Saturday and cool sounds other nights in a large, airy interior.

The southwest coast

The southwest Algarve is less built-up than the central stretch. The lush Mediterranean-type vegetation gives way to coarser Atlantic scrub and grassland; it's a highly scenic area of gently rolling hills, clifftop walks and remote coves. The coast has just three resorts, of which Luz is the most upmarket. Neighbouring Burgau marks the eastern boundary of the Parque Natural do Sudoeste Alentejano e Costa Vicentina, a natural park set up to protect the coast from further development. Bustling in summer, Burgau and neighbouring Salema retain vestiges of their former status as fishing villages, while nearby, you can still find quiet, isolated beaches around Figueira, Raposeira and Vila do Bispo.

Luz

Around 6 daily buses from Lagos.

Towered over by high cliffs and fronted with a wide crescent of sandy beach, the village of Luz is beautifully situated. It has no real centre as such; white chalets, villas, pools and tennis courts cluster behind the beach, but the development is generally low-rise and attracts well-heeled families, mostly British. Buses from Lagos drop you a block back from the church, from where it's a short walk downhill to the attractive palm-lined beachside promenade with its cafés, restaurants and souvenir stalls. Between May and September its proximity to Lagos means the beach gets packed, and holidaymakers take to the water with pedaloes, banana boats and the like. Outside summer the beach is quiet and most of its beachside restaurants close down. Swimming is best at the western end of the

▼ LUZ SEAFRONT PROMENADE

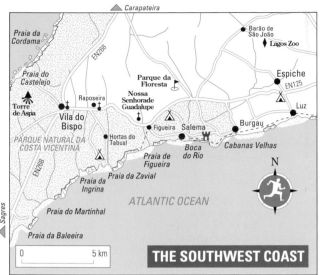

Carapateira

Barão de
São João

Lagos Zoo

Praia da
Cordama

Espiche

EN125

Praia do
Castelejo

Parque da
Floresta

Luz

Nossa
Senhora de
Guadalupe

Raposeira

Torre
de Aspa

Vila do
Bispo

Figueira Salema

Burgau

PARQUE NATURAL DA
COSTA VICENTINA

Hortas do
Tabual

Boca
do Rio

Cabanas Velhas

N

Praia de
Figueira

Praia da Zavial

EN268

Praia da
Ingrina

ATLANTIC OCEAN

Praia do Martinhal

Praia da Baleeira

0   5 km

THE SOUTHWEST COAST

Sagres

sands; the other end, below the dramatic cliffs, becomes more rocky. The promenade continues west from the beach above a rocky foreshore. Here you'll find the walled-off **Ruínas Romanos** (daily 10am–5pm; free), where excavations reveal the skant remains of a Roman house (dating from the third to fifth centuries), fish-preserving tanks and a bathhouse. The promenade wends its way to the town's pretty church and an old fort, now a restaurant (see p.162). West of here lies an attractive smaller beach, backed by weirdly sculpted sandstone – some of it carved into by artistic visitors.

Luz coastal walks

There are some excellent coast walks within reach of Luz. The easiest of these is a walk to the triangulation point obelisk (*atalaia, 109m*) on the clifftop to the east of Luz, a forty-minute round trip which offers splendid views of the coast. To get there, follow the road that runs east and parallel to the beach. At the edge of town you'll see a cobbled track heading uphill. The track becomes a dirt path as you head up a very steep hillside towards the obelisk, clearly visible ahead of you. If you want to walk further, you can continue along the coast path from here all the way to Porto de Mós (1hr) and Lagos (a further 45min), an exhilarating and breezy clifftop walk with striking views towards Ponta da Piedade (see p.151), though it becomes increasingly built-up from Porto de Mós on.

A shorter but equally bracing walk from Luz is to head west along the coast path to Burgau (1hr). From the beachside promenade pass the fort and take the first left at *The Bull* pub, continuing straight on until the road turns into a track. The track runs parallel to the coast until you reach Burgau, offering more superb views over the sea and back towards town. You can catch a bus back to Luz from Burgau.

▲ BURGAU

Burgau

Around 6 daily buses from Lagos.
Burgau is a handsome little resort of narrow cobbled lanes which tumble down a steep hillside to a fine sandy beach set below low cliffs. Fishing is still a going concern here and boats line the lower roads, which double up as slipways, while narrow alleys weave around to a *miradouro* offering fine views over the sands. In July and August the village is somewhat mobbed, when its surrounding villas are chock-a-block, but it retains a distinct character, with locals cooking fish on tiny grills outside their homes.

Boca do Rio

Set below the ruins of a seventeenth-century fortress in a broad, flat river valley, Boca do Rio ("mouth of the river") is an unspoilt bay strewn with giant boulders. Once this was an important Roman settlement, and many

of the remains at Lagos's Museu Regional were found at this spot. The bay is a popular spot for campervanners, and at low tide sands are revealed, making it a decent swimming spot.

Parque da Floresta

Just off the EN125, by the village of Budens, you'll see the extensive grounds of the Parque da Floresta (☎282 690 007, ⓦwww.parquedafloresta.com), a huge sports centre and holiday village complex set round the western Algarve's main golf course and boasting a pool, spa, tennis courts, restaurants and kids' entertainment programme.

Salema

6–8 daily buses from Lagos and Sagres. Approached via a delightful, cultivated valley, the small fishing village of Salema has a long stretch of beach and a low-key charm that makes it popular with independent travellers. Buses stop just above the beach, where brightly coloured boats are still hauled up for the day. The atmospheric old centre extends east from the bus stop, a network of narrow alleys and whitewashed fishermen's houses, many now given over to inexpensive holiday lets: just stroll round and look for the signs, or ask at the local bars if you want to stay.

Burgau–Salema walk

You can walk to Salema from Burgau (1hr 30min) along a clifftop coastal path, which begins west of Burgau. There are excellent views back up the coast towards Lagos and you can stop off at a series of remote bays, including Cabanas Velhas and Boca do Rio (see above). The coast path eventually joins the road winding down to Salema.

▲ SALEMA BEACH

Figueira and Praia da Figueira

Regular buses from Lagos and Sagres; some stop on the main EN125, a short walk from Figueira. The best way to appreciate some of the unspoilt coastal countryside of the southwest Algarve is to take the path to the beach of Praia da Figueira. This is a fine bay – often deserted except for a few naturists – with the sparse remains of a fort on the hill above. The delightful 25-minute walk starts in Figueira, a small agricultural village whose surrounding fields are still tilled by mules. Clearly signed, the track heads down beside a river through farmland, passing traditional wells. The path narrows, following a river overgrown with wild thyme and fennel. To get to the beach, cross the shallow stream at the end.

Nossa Senhora de Guadalupe

Between Figueira and Raposeira, a sign points off the main EN125 to the chapel of Nossa Senhora de Guadalupe, a squat, dark-stoned church reached via the old road which runs parallel to the highway.

Built in the thirteenth century by the Knights Templar and said to have been frequented by Henry the Navigator, the chapel stands in rural solitude. It is usually kept locked, but it's a pleasant place to stroll around or have a picnic.

Raposeira, Praia do Zavial and Praia da Ingrina

Henry the Navigator is believed to have lived for a while in the small rural village of Raposeira, an attractive enough place with a handsome church. However, the village is sliced through by the highway, and there's not much reason to come here except to turn off the road to a couple of fine beaches. Praia do Zavial is a small bay below low cliffs, a popular spot with surfers thanks to its large breakers (swimmers should take care of undertows). For calmer swimming, continue down the road another kilometre round the bay to Praia da Ingrina, a small sandy cove, good for beachcombing amid the rock pools.

Vila do Bispo

Vila do Bispo is a fairly traditional, if run-down, Algarve village with a core of old white houses. It is centred on a lovely seventeenth-century parish church (Mon–Sat 10am–1pm &

▼ PRAIA DO ZAVIAL

2–6pm), every interior surface of which has been painted, tiled or gilded. In September the town holds a highly atmospheric agricultural expo, where crusty farm folk enjoy food stalls and music; at other times it makes a pleasant spot for a coffee or a meal.

Praia do Castelejo

One of the area's best beaches is Praia do Castelejo, reached via Vila do Bispo – from the main square, take the road downhill past the post office, turn left and then bear right – along a narrow road leading 5km west. It crosses a stretch of bleak moors and hills, and the final approach is down a winding and precipitous descent. But it is worth the effort: the beach is a huge swathe of sand (which can be covered in high tides) lashed by heavy waves below dark-grey cliffs. The beach has an edge-of-the-world feel, though the beachside café (closed Wed & Oct–April) adds a slight touch of civilization.

Accommodation

Hotel Belavista da Luz

Urbanização da Belavista, Luz ☏ 282 788 655, ⓦ belavistadaluz.com. Around 1km uphill on the road towards Sagres, this pink, modern four-star lacks character but is the best option for comfort, offering a restaurant, pool, tennis courts, gym and health club, and it has disabled access. €150.

Casa Grande

Burgau ☏ 282 697 416, ⓦ nexus -pt.com/casagrande. On the road towards Luz, this characterful, English-run manor house is set in its own grounds and fronted by a spiky dragon tree. There are giant rooms with soaring ceilings, each decorated with a motley assortment of period furniture. Upstairs rooms are largest with their own balconies (€80). Book ahead in high season as there are only a handful of rooms. €40.

▼ PRAIA DO CASTELEJO

A Mare

Salema ☎282 695 165, ⓦalgarve
.co.uk. On the hill above the
main road into town, this good-
value and attractively renovated
house has a lovely sea-facing
terrace and an airy breakfast
room. En-suite rooms are tiny
but spotless. Price does not
include breakfast. €67.

Ocean Villas

Rua da Calheta 38, Luz ☎916 975
621, UK bookings ☎01844 238638,
ⓦwww.starvilla.com. In the quieter,
west part of Luz, a series of
tasteful low-rise villas and
apartments clusters round a
central courtyard with its own
elongated pool, Jacuzzi and
barbecue area. The front villas
overlook a rocky foreshore
(and quiet road) and all are well
equipped with terraces and sun
loungers. No breakfast. One
week lets from €850.

Hotel Praia do Burgau

Rua da Fortaleza, Burgau ☎282 690
160, ℮imulagos@sapo.pt. On a
hillside to the east of town,
this modern three-star was
built with environmentally
neutral, non-toxic materials.
Decent-sized rooms have their
own minibars and satellite TV.
The top rooms (€15 extra)
have balconies with superb
views, and there's also a small
pool. €110.

Hotel Residencial Salema

Rua 28 de Janeiro, Salema ☎282
665 328, ⓦhotelsalema.com.
Closed Nov–Feb. Plonked rather
unceremoniously by the
cobbled square just back from
the beach, this modern block
offers decent accommodation
in small rooms, some with their
own balconies with skewed sea
views. There's also a bar and TV
room. €90.

Campsites

Quinta dos Carriços

Quinta dos Carriços, Salema ☎282
695 201, ℮quintacarrico@oninet
.pt. An excellent campsite with
landscaped grounds, beautifully
positioned 1.5km from Salema
up towards the main highway
– the bus passes on the way
into the village. It's well
equipped with a mini market,
restaurant, bar, launderette and
even a car wash.

Praia da Ingrina

Praia da Ingrina ☎ & ℉282 639 242.
Around 1km inland from Praia
da Ingrina, this basic campsite
sits in a lovely rural setting.
Limited facilities include a small
shop and an attractive bar-
restaurant.

Valverde

Luz ☎282 789 211, ⓦwww.orbitur
.pt. An attractive leafy campsite
1.5km from Luz. Close to the
highway, with a full range of
tourist facilities including a
kids' playground, restaurant,
supermarket and bar.

Shops

Hipercerâmica Paraíso

EN125, Raposeira. Daily 9.30am–7pm.
On the western fringes of
Raposeira, this is a great place
for browsing for ceramics.
There's genuine quality amongst
some cheap tat – persevere and
you'll find some fine mugs, cups,
plates, bowls and dishes.

Cafés

Brizze

Rua 25 Abril, Burgau. Daily 8am–
midnight. A small café-bar with

a series of outdoor terraces on Burgau's steepest beachside approach. It's a great stop for a coffee, snack or an evening beer.

Kiwi Pastelaria

Avenida dos Pescadores, Luz. Daily 9am–10pm. Right on the beachside promenade, the outdoor tables offer an ideal breakfast stop, with fresh croissants, fruit juices and coffee. It also serves a good range of ice creams, salads and sandwiches.

Restaurants

Adega Casa Grande

Burgau ☎282 697 416. Mon–Fri 7–11pm, closed Nov. Attached to the *Casa Grande* guesthouse (see p.160), this bar-restaurant is set in an atmospheric former wine cellar (*adega*). It offers great, inexpensive Portuguese grills and international dishes such as chicken curry, and there are some vegetarian options, too.

A Barraca

Largo dos Pescadores 2, Burgau ☎282 697 748. Daily noon–3pm & 7–10pm. This clifftop restaurant is a top spot for mid-priced meat dishes and seafood (around €8–12), including the speciality, *cataplanas*. It's best in summer since, at other times, plastic sheets over the terrace put paid to the wind and also the views.

Beach Bar Burgau

Praia de Burgau ☎282 697 553. Restaurant: Tues–Sun noon–3pm & 7–10pm; bar: April–Oct Mon 9.30am–7pm, Tues–Sun 9.30am–2am; Nov–March Tues–Sun noon–3pm. A restaurant-bar with a splendid terrace on the beach. It's best to reserve to be guaranteed an evening table. The fish and grills are slightly

pricey but well presented. Alternatively, enjoy a beer or five at its late-opening bar.

Boia Bar

Rua das Pescadores 101, Salema ☎282 695 382. Daily 10.30am–2am. On the edge of the old centre facing the beach, this smart, modern restaurant does a good range of tasty if pricey fish; the superb *caldeirada* (fish stew) for four is the speciality.

Correia

Rua 1º de Maio, Vila do Bispo. Mon–Fri & Sun 1–3pm & 7–10pm. Very much off the tourist circuit, just down from the church, this attractive, roomy restaurant has *azulejos* on the walls and a good-value menu of delicious grilled meats and fish (meals around €15).

The Dolphin

Rua da Calheta 14a, Luz. Mon–Sat 4–11pm. A modern first-floor restaurant offering meaty South African cuisine including steaks and venison from around €14. There are a few Portuguese dishes, too, while the adventurous can sample ostrich schnitzel. Good sea views and snappy service.

Fortaleza da Luz

Rua da Igreja 3, Luz ☎282 789 926. Daily noon–3pm & 7–9.30pm. The Fortaleza (castle) is the most upmarket choice in Luz, with pricey top-notch pasta dishes, omelettes and Algarvian dishes, such as pork Monchique-style and delicious *bolo de amendôa* (almond cake). There are tables on the grassy terrace, and its ornate dining room offers superb sea views; there's also live music at weekends, usually Sunday-lunch jazz.

Mira Mar

Trav Mira Mar 6, Salema ☎919 560 339. Daily 12.30–3pm & 7–11pm. A small, simple but very welcoming restaurant right on the beach. Excellent and well-priced fresh fish – the bream is superb – is served on a little terrace facing the waves. The house wine or sangria is good value, too. Around €15 for a full meal.

O Poço

Avda dos Pescadores, Luz ☎282 789 189. Daily 12.30–3pm & 7–10pm. "The well" boasts a prime spot overlooking the sands and the beachside promenade. The reasonably priced seafood and meat dishes include an excellent *espadarte de tamboril* (monkfish kebab). Get here early to bag a window seat, or reserve in advance.

Sebastião

Praia da Ingrina. Mon & Wed–Sun 11am–10pm. A little stone beachside café-restaurant where you can tuck into filling grills (around €15) or enjoy drinks on a palm-shaded terrace facing the waves.

Zavial

Praia do Zavial ☎282 639 282. Tues–Sun noon–5pm & 7–10pm. Set in a modern stone building with a beach-facing terrace, this beach restaurant serves a decent range of pricey but tasty grilled meat and fish. There's also inexpensive baguettes and a special kids' menu.

Bars

Aventura

Rua das Pescadores 80, Salema. Daily 9am–2am. An atmospheric French-owned bar on the road into the old village, attracting a young crowd.

The Bull

Rua da Calheta 5, Luz ☎282 788 823. Daily 10.30am–3am. Just up from the fort, this English-style pub has a range of drinks, English breakfasts and inexpensive pub grub firmly geared to British tastes. There's an outdoor terrace with fine views, but it's liveliest when everyone crams inside for the latest soccer game on TV.

Veranda

Largo dos Pescadores 4, Burgau. Daily 9am–midnight. A lively café-bar with a fine terrace overlooking the old town and sea. Good fruit shakes, breakfasts and boppy sounds.

Sagres and around

Teetering on the edge of the continent, Sagres is the southwesternmost harbour in Europe. It extends along a clifftop above a working fishing harbour, and although it is a straggling, ungainly town, its dramatic position and proximity to superb beaches attract substantial summer crowds. At other times it's popular with surfers, lured by superb waves and various surf schools. Numerous day-trippers also pass through here to see Cabo de São Vicente, a dramatic lighthouse-capped headland, and the village's imposing fortress, believed to have been Prince Henry the Navigator's school of navigation. On 15 August – Sagres' lively Saint's Day – the town celebrates with music, dancing and fireworks.

Praça da República

Praça da República is the main focus of the town, an attractive cobbled space lined with squat palms and whitewashed cafés. At the end of the day, the elderly gather at the dusty square alongside the tourist office to play games of boules.

The Fortaleza

Daily: May–Sept 10am–8pm; Oct–April 9.30am–5.30pm. €3. The white walls of Sagres' Fortaleza (fortress) dominate the clifftops southwest of the village. An immense circuit of walls once surrounded this vast, shelf-like promontory, high above the Atlantic. What you see today was largely rebuilt in 1793: only the north side survives intact, the rest destroyed in the 1755 earthquake.

The entrance is through a formidable rock tunnel, before which is spread a huge pebble wind compass known as the **Rosa dos Ventos** (wind rose), unearthed beneath a church in 1921 and used to measure the direction of the wind. Its 43-

SAGRES & AROUND

metre diameter is divided into forty segments made of stone, radiating out like spokes on a bike wheel. No one is sure whether the compass dates back to Henry's time, though the simple, much-restored chapel of **Nossa Senhora da Graça** beside the compass is accepted as dating from the fifteenth century.

Visiting Sagres

Buses from Lagos stop by Sagres' main Praça da República and continue down to the harbour. At the back of the square, in the *Residencial Dom Henrique*, you'll find a privately run tourist office, Turinfo (daily 8am–midnight; ☎282 620 003, ☎282 620 004), which can arrange room rental, book you on a boat tour, rent out mountain bikes, organize surf lessons and offer Internet access. The main turismo, at Rua 25 de Abril 26–28 (Mon–Fri: May–Sept 9.30am–12.30pm & 2–6pm; Oct–April 9.30am–12.30pm & 1.30–5.30pm; ☎282 624 873), hands free town maps and bus timetables.

A cluster of modern buildings faces the fortress walls – a shop, café and exhibition space showing maps of Portugal and other nautical memorabilia – but, gracelessly constructed with concrete, they've done little to enhance the beauty of the site. However, it's lovely to wander around the walls and out to Ponta de Sagres, a headland with a small lighthouse beacon offering fine views up and down the coast, past precariously balanced fishermen dangling their lines off the immense cliffs.

Praia da Mareta and Praia de Tonel

Most of Sagres' excellent beaches are within easy walking distance of the town. The nearest (and therefore most crowded) beach, Praia da Mareta, is a lovely stretch of soft sand just five minutes' walk downhill southeast from Praça da República. Out towards the fortress, Praia de Tonel is another superb sandy beach below cliffs, popular with surfers: take great care when swimming, as the undertow can be fierce.

Porto da Baleeira

Sagres' atmospheric Porto da Baleeira ("port of the whaleboats") is an earthy working harbour, lined with boat-building yards and fishing boats – watching the day's catch come in is always something of an event. You can also arrange boat trips from here to Cabo de São Vicente (around €20) and dolphin-watching (€30), or book diving courses (from €35).

Prince Henry's School of Navigation

Henry developed thirteenth-century fortifications at Sagres to form a secure base for his seafaring academy, and spent the last three years of his life working in the Fortaleza from his home in Sagres. Here, the Prince gathered some of the greatest astronomers, cartographers and adventurers of his age. Fernão de Magalhães (Magellan), Pedro Álvares Cabral and Vasco da Gama all studied at Sagres, and from the beach at Beliche – midway between the capes of Sagres and São Vicente – the first caravels were launched, revolutionizing shipping with their wide hulls, small adaptable sails, and ability to sail close to the wind. Each year new expeditions were dispatched to penetrate a little further into the unknown, and to resolve the great navigational enigma presented by the west coast of Africa, thereby laying the foundations of the country's overseas empire.

EATING & DRINKING						
Água Salgado	2	A Grelha	6	Rosa dos	
Bossa Nova	5	Last Chance		Ventos	7
Bubble Lounge	1	Saloon	11	A Tasca	10
Casa Sagres	B	Mar á Vista	8	Vila Velha	9
Dromedário	4	Marreiros	3		
Fiodepesca	13	Raposo	12		

ACCOMMODATION	
Alojamento Particular	C
Baleeira	A
Casa Sagres	B
Dom Henrique	D
Orquídea	E
Pousada do Infante	F

Praia do Martinhal

A ten-minute walk along the clifftop from above the harbour leads to Praia do Martinhal, a wide sandy crescent that is generally quieter than the other beaches, despite a large new building development. It is backed by beachside cafés, a marshy lagoon and a windsurfing school (☏282 624 147), which can also organize kite-surfing.

Praia de Beliche

Out on the road to Cabo de São Vicente, with correspondingly fewer crowds, Praia de Beliche (or Belixe) is where Henry the Navigator's caravels first set off to explore the unknown world; little can have changed here since, and you are usually guaranteed plenty of sand to yourself. The beach, set beneath steep cliffs, is overlooked by a small fortress, once a restaurant and

pousada, but currently closed for safety reasons.

Cabo de São Vicente

The wild headland of Cabo de São Vicente is the southwesternmost point of the Iberian peninsula. Known as Promontorium Sacrum, the headland was sacred to the Romans, who believed the sun sank hissing into the water beyond here every night. Legend has it that in the eighth century, Christians took the remains of Saint Vincent with them from Spain as they fled the invading Moors. They arrived at the safe outpost of the cape, where they later built a chapel to house his bones, though these were later moved to Lisbon.

Today the only buildings to be seen are the ruins of a sixteenth-century Capuchin monastery and a nineteenth-century lighthouse, which has the most powerful beam in

▲ WINDSURFERS, PRAIA DO MARTINHAL

Europe. The cape is a dramatic and exhilarating six-kilometre walk from Sagres, with a cliff path skirting the vertiginous drop for much of the way. Walking on the road is easier if slightly less scenic – it'll take less than an hour and a half, with glorious views all the way. Try to be at the cape for sunset, which is invariably gorgeous, though frequently windy. Today the sea off this wild set of cliffs shelters the highest concentration of marine life in Portugal, and it is also rich in bird life: at various times of year you should be able to spot blue rock thrushes and peregrine falcons nesting on the cliffs along with rare birds such as Bonelli's eagles, white storks, rock doves, kites and white herons.

Accommodation

Alojamento Particular

Praça da República 1–5, Sagres ☎282 624 096, ✉alojamento.particular @netvisao.pt. Simple but good-value private rooms right on the main square in a tall town house. Ask for the top-floor room if available, which comes complete with balcony facing

the sea. There's no breakfast, but the town's best cafés are opposite. €45.

Casa Sagres

Praça da República, Sagres ☎282 624 358. Behind the main square on the road down to Praia da Mareta, this is primarily a restaurant that also lets out decent en-suite rooms. The best ones have sea-facing balconies (€10 extra). €60.

Residencial Dom Henrique

Praça da República, Sagres ☎282 620 000, ⬡domhenrique.com. In a

▲ LIGHTHOUSE AT CABO DE SÃO VICENTE

▲ SAGRES' PORTO DA BALEEIRA

perfect position on the main square and with a terrace offering wonderful sea views, this is a good first port of call. There's an airy bar, and rooms have bath and satellite TV; rooms with sea-facing balconies cost €86, otherwise €78.

Orquídea

Sítio da Baleeira, Sagres ☎ 282 624 257, ⓦ veloz-plus.com. Simple but spacious and good-value one- and two-bedroom apartments with kitchenettes in an ungainly concrete block that's superbly positioned above the harbour with great sea views. Facilities include a pool and tennis courts. €70.

Pousada do Infante

Sagres ☎ 282 620 240, ⓦ www .pousadas.pt. An attractive and highly characterful clifftop mansion with Moorish elements and splendid views over the sea. Rooms are large, with terraces or balconies. The clifftop garden boasts a swimming pool and tennis courts, while inside there's a games room, bar and restaurant. €175.

Campsite

Parque de Campismo de Sagres

Cerro das Moitos ☎ 282 624 351, ⓦ www.orbitur.pt. Two kilometres northwest of the village, this rather exposed campsite has a pleasing rural setting, though facilities are limited.

Cafés

Pastelaria Marreiros

Praça da República 12, Sagres. Daily 8am–8pm. A very popular spot, thanks to the attractive outside tables on the main square, offering a good range of snacks, including croissants, *tostas* and sandwiches.

Nortada

Praia da Martinhal. Daily: May–Oct 10am–midnight; Sept–April Mon & Wed–Thurs 11am–5pm. A bleached-wood beach bar and café with a terrace right on the sands. It serves a good range of mid-priced international dishes along with the usual Portuguese fare and baguettes; it also does fine milkshakes and fresh juices, and is the base for the local watersports school.

Restaurants

Bossa Nova

Rua Comandante Matoso 8650, Sagres ☏ 282 624 566. Tues–Sun noon–11pm. A quietly trendy place set in former stables, noted for its eclectic mix of dishes; choose from the excellent, good-value pizzas, pasta, salads and imaginative vegetarian meals. There are a few tables in the inner courtyard.

Fiodepesca

Rua Infante Dom Henriques, Sagres ☏ 282 620 280. Mon–Wed & Fri–Sun 5–11pm. A classy upmarket newcomer offering an interesting mixture of traditional Portuguese fare and world cuisine, including Sagres Thai (prawns with noodle salad), spaghetti with salmon and duck with Cognac sauce. Mains around €15.

A Grelha

Rua Comandante Matoso, Sagres ☏ 282 624 193. Daily noon–3pm & 6–10pm. A simple grill house run by old-timers who are never hurried. Meat and fish are good value and the chicken piri-piri is superb. Under €15 for a full meal.

Mar á Vista

Sítio da Mareta, Sagres ☏ 282 624 247. Mon, Tues & Thurs–Sun 10am–midnight. On a scrubby patch of ground just off the road to Praia da Mareta, this pleasant eatery serves a long list of good-value fish, omelettes and salads (around €15 for a full meal), with fine views from its outdoor tables.

Raposo

Praia da Mareta ☏ 282 624 168. Daily 10am–10pm. A lovely beach bar-restaurant right on the sands, filled with surfers during the day. Most of the meat dishes are good value, although the seafood is expensive.

A Tasca

Porto da Baleeira, Sagres ☏ 282 624 177. May–Sept daily 8am–midnight; Oct–April closed Sat. Very popular with tour groups and expensive, this is nevertheless the best of Sagres' fish restaurants, with

▲ SAGRES HARBOUR

a few meat dishes and superb fish straight from the harbour. Tables outside face the Atlantic, though it's just as fun in the barn-like interior, its walls encrusted with pebbles and old bottles. Expect to pay upwards of €30.

Vila Velha
Rua Patrão A. Faustino, Sagres ☎282 624 788. May–Sept daily 6.30–10pm; Oct–April Tues–Sun 6.30–10pm. In a pretty white house, this upmarket and somewhat formal restaurant serves superior dishes that blend new and traditional Portuguese cuisine, including *tagliatelle com camarão e tamboril* (pasta with shrimp and monkfish). There is usually a vegetarian option, a children's menu and superb crepes for dessert. Booking is advised. Around €25 for a full meal.

Bars

Água Salgado
Rua Comandante Matoso, Sagres. Daily 10am–3am. A bright bar with a happening feel to it, with cool sounds and table football. Along with drinks it serves crepes and pizzas.

Bubble Lounge
Rua Nossa Senhora da Graça, Sagres. May–Sept daily 9am–2am; Oct–April Tues–Sun 6pm–2am. A laid-back surfers' bar with comfy chairs, a screen showing the day's surf moves, games, books and ambient sounds. Occasional live music, too.

Dromedário
Rua Comandante Matoso, Sagres. Mon & Wed–Sun 10am–2am. A great little bar with Egyptian-inspired decor, attracting a young clientele. It serves a mean range of cocktails and juices, along with inexpensive snacks and great breakfasts. Live jazz and karaoke on some nights.

Last Chance Saloon
Sítio da Mareta, Sagres. Tues–Sun 6pm–midnight. In a wooden shack overlooking the beach, this is a laid-back place to down an early-evening beer or two as the sun sets.

Rosa dos Ventos
Praça da República, Sagres. Mon & Wed–Sun noon–midnight. An atmospheric bar in an old town house on the main square, which also does simple food including vegetarian options.

▲ LAST CHANCE SALOON, SAGRES

The west coast

The Algarve's west coast faces the full brunt of the Atlantic, whose crashing breakers and cooler waters have deterred developers. This is popular territory for surfers, hardy nudists who appreciate the remote beaches, and campervanners, but be warned that the sea can be dangerous and swimmers should take great care. The rocky coastline is punctuated by fantastic broad beaches accessible from the small village of Carrapateira, or the prettier and livelier Aljezur and Odeceixe. The designation in 1995 of this entire stretch of coast as a nature reserve – the Parque Natural Sudoeste Alentejano e Costa Vincentina – has restricted development, though this means there is a paucity of accommodation. Public transport serves the main centres, but most of these are set back from the beaches, so having your own transport is a distinct advantage.

Carrapateira and its beaches

Connected by 2 weekday buses from Vila do Bispo. Set in gently rolling countryside studded with aromatic pine and eucalyptus, Carrapateira is a fairly nondescript village that's little more than a cluster of houses round a hilltop church. Its main appeal is its location – just 3km from **Praia da Bordeira**, one of the best beaches in the entire Algarve. In contrast to the craggy, cliff-backed beaches further south, this spectacular deep stretch of sands spills inland to merge with dunes and the wide river valley behind. The road west from Carrapateira passes a small car park next to the river, from where you cross a narrow stretch of the water on to the back of the beach. Alternatively, carry on up the hill where another car park sits just above the sands. It's a beautiful spot, popular with families.

Four kilometres south of Praia da Bordeira, along the coast

THE WEST COAST

ATLANTIC OCEAN

N

Praia de Odeceixe
Odeceixe
Maria Vinagre
Rogil
Praia Amoreira
Praia de Monte Clérigo
Aljezur
Igreja Nova
Vale da Telha
Praia da Arrifana
Barranco da Vaca
Praia de Vale de Figueiras
Praia da Bordeira
Carrapateira
Praia do Amado

PARQUE NATURAL DA COSTA VICENTINA
SERRA DE ESPINHAÇO DE CÃO
EN268
Monchique

0   5 km

Sagres

road, lies **Praia do Amado**, which is also signed off the main road just south of Carrapateira. Another fantastic, broad sandy bay backed by low hills with a couple of seasonal cafés, this one is particularly popular with surfers. There's a surf school here

▲ PRAIA DO AMADO

(☎ 282 624 560, ⓦ algarve
.surfcamp.com; daily 10.30am–
dusk, weather permitting), which
offers equipment hire and surf
courses from €35.

Aljezur

The village of Aljezur is both the
prettiest and liveliest town along
the west coast of the Algarve.
It is divided into three distinct
parts. The main coast road passes
through a prosaic, modern
lower town with banks, the
post office and a range of cafés
and restaurants. Uphill, towards
Monchique, lies Igreja Nova,
a pleasant if functional suburb
which takes its name from the
"new church" that was built here
after the 1755 earthquake in the
belief that the residents would
move away from the original
settlement, though in fact most
people preferred to stay put.

The most interesting part of
town is the historic old town
beyond the bridge over the
Aljezur river – a network of
narrow cobbled streets
reaching up between
whitewashed houses to the
remains of a tenth-century
Moorish **castle**. It's a lovely
walk to the castle, with
sweeping views over the valley.

Aljezur's museums

Mon–Fri 9.30am–1pm & 2.30–5.30pm.
€2, tickets available from Museu
Municipal. Aljezur has a number

of museums – you can buy
a ticket, valid for all of them,
at the **Museu Municipal** on
Largo 5 de Outubro, set in
the attractive former town
hall. This houses an eclectic
collection of historical artefacts
gathered from the region: dusty
farm implements, old axes and
the like. At quiet times, you
have to ask for access to the
town's other museums which
are usually locked. The best
of these is the **Casa Museu
Pintor José Cercas**, up the
hill on Rua do Castelo, which
displays the works of local artist
José Cercas, who lived in the
house until his death in 1992.
His well-observed landscapes
and religious scenes are
complemented by an attractive
house with a pretty garden.

Arrifana

Served by 2 daily buses from Aljezur
(May–Sept only). One kilometre
south of Aljezur, a road heads
down to the longest beach on
this stretch – at Arrifana, 10km
to the southeast. The beach is
a fine sandy sweep set below
high, crumbling black cliffs. A
narrow road gives access to the
beach, but in high season all
car-parking spots are usually
taken, which means parking at
the top of the cliff, a steep five-
minute walk away. The beach
is popular with surfers, and surf
competitions are sometimes

Visiting Aljezur

There are 4 buses daily to Aljezur from Lagos via Bensafrim, continuing to Odeceixe. A further 3 buses run daily from Lagos via Portimão to Aljezur, continuing on to Lisbon. The turismo (May–Sept Mon & Fri–Sun 9.30am–12.30pm & 2–6pm, Tues–Thurs 9.30am–7pm; Oct–April Mon & Fri–Sun 9.30am–1pm & 2–5.30pm, Tues–Thurs 9.30am–5.30pm; ☏ 282 998 229) is in Largo do Mercado, by the river and in front of the town market.

held here. The clifftop boasts the remains of a ruined fort, just up from a cluster of cafés and holiday villas.

Monte Clérigo

Served by 2 daily buses from Aljezur (May–Sept only). Monte Clérigo is a pretty little holiday village of pink- and white-faced beach houses. A cluster of café-restaurants looks onto a superb, family-oriented beach tucked into the foot of a river valley.

Praia Amoreira

The quiet beach of Praia Amoreira is another fine, sandy bay extending north of the mouth of the Riba de Aljezur. The beach is accessible off the main Aljezur–Odeceixe road, some 5km northwest of Aljezur (no public transport connections), and the drive here down a broad river valley is delightful. There's a handy seasonal beach café.

Odeceixe

Served by 2–3 daily buses from Lagos. The attractive town of Odeceixe tumbles down a hillside opposite the broad valley of the Odeceixe river below the winding, tree-lined main coast road. Sleepy out of season, its character changes in summer when it attracts a steady stream of surfers, campervanners and families, lured by the local beach (see below). Most of the action is centred on the pedestrianized main square, Largo 1º de Maio, from where the beach is signed to the west. Round here you'll find the market, post office, banks, supermarkets and plenty of places letting out rooms.

Praia de Odeceixe

Served by road-train, roughly hourly, June–Aug only, €1 return. The broad, sandy bay of Praia de Odeceixe lies some 4km to the west of the village of Odeceixe

▼ PRAIA DA ARRIFANA

PLACES

The west coast

▲ PRAIA DE ODECEIXE

and is reached via a verdant river valley. It's a lovely walk along the river to the beach. Framed by low cliffs, it is one of the most sheltered beaches on this stretch of coast, offering superb surfing and relatively safe swimming, especially at low tide, or you can splash about in the river itself. A pretty cluster of traditional houses and cafés lies banked up to the south of the bay, though as most are holiday homes it's closed up and largely deserted out of season. A small turismo kiosk above the beach can help out if you need advice on accommodation or transport (Mon–Fri 9.30–noon & 3–4pm; ☏961 624 596).

Accommodation

Casa Hospedes Celeste

Rua Nova 9, Odeceixe ☏282 947 150. ⓦwww.casaceleste.web.pt. An attractive, traditional town house with spacious rooms in the heart of Odeceixe. It's best to avoid the downstairs rooms, though, or you'll feel like you're sleeping in the street. €60.

Residencial Dom Sancho

Largo Igreja Nova 1, Igreja Nova, Aljezur ☏282 997 070, ⓔturimol @mail.telepac.pt. This modern guesthouse sits just above the main church overlooking a pedestrianized street. Rooms are large and comfortable, with bath and TV. €55.

Dorita

Praia de Odeceixe ☏282 947 581. Closed Nov–April. Simple rooms, the best with sweeping views over the waves, are let out by the restaurant (see opposite) above the beach. One even has a terrace. Those with private bath are €10 extra. Price does not include breakfast. Book ahead in high season. €50.

Pensão das Dunas

Rua da Padaria 9, Carrapateira ☏ & ⒻAX 282 973 118. A very pretty building on the beach-side of the village, this has a number of simple rooms overlooking a flower-filled courtyard, and there are apartments for two or four people. The price includes a substantial breakfast. Rooms €30, apartments €45–65.

Oceano

Arrifana ☎ 282 997 300. Restaurant closed Tues. A friendly, all-purpose café, restaurant and guesthouse on the clifftop above the beach. Pleasant rooms come with shower and fine views, while the downstairs restaurant does fine mid-priced fish and grills. Price does not include breakfast. €30.

Residêncio do Parque

Rua do Correiro 15, Odeceixe ☎ 282 947 117. Run by an eccentric but very welcoming owner, this huge house has a mixed bag of rooms – the best on the top floor with small balconies overlooking the valley; all are en suite with TVs, while the downstairs bar is usually lively and fun. Huge off-season reductions. €62.

Campsite

Serrão

Herdade do Serrão, Aljezur ☎ 282 990 220, ⊜ camping-serrao@clix.pt. This large, tranquil campsite is set amongst dense trees some 7km northwest of Aljezur. It has its own pool, supermarket and tennis courts.

Café

Pastelaria Mioto

Rua 25 de Abril, Loja H, Aljezur ☎ 282 998 803. Daily 6am–midnight. A neat, modern *pastelaria* tucked into the back of a shopping centre. It offers a fine range of cakes and pastries, but the main appeal is a superb terrace overlooking the verdant river valley behind.

Restaurants

Dorita

Praia de Odeceixe ☎ 282 947 581. Daily 10am–10pm, closed Nov–April. On the road above the beach, this simple café-restaurant offers mid-priced Portuguese food best enjoyed on the outside terrace overlooking the beach. It also lets out rooms (see opposite).

Pont'a Pé

Largo da Liberdade 16, Aljezur ☎ 282 998 104. Mon–Sat 12.30–3pm & 7–11pm. Moderately priced grills are served at this cosy diner up by the tourist office. It also has an appealing riverside terrace complete with table football. Live music most weekends competes with the sound of the resident frogs.

PLACES The west coast

▼ MONTE CLÉRIGO

▲ ALJEZUR OLD TOWN

O Retiro do Adelino

Rua Nova 20, Odeceixe ☎ 282 947 352. Tues–Sun noon–3pm & 6–11pm. Bumper portions of inexpensive grilled chicken, fish with tomato rice and *feijoada* are served at this friendly grill house with a little courtyard. It also does fine traditional dishes such as rabbit stew and beans with prawns from around €8.

Ruth O Ivo

Rua 25 de Abril 14, Aljezur ☎ 282 998 534. Mon–Fri & Sun noon–3pm & 6–11pm. This highly regarded restaurant specializes in moderately priced regional dishes, including the local speciality, goose barnacles with sweet potatoes. Also recommended is the superb *arroz de tamboril com camarão* (monkfish and prawn rice).

O Sitio do Rio

Praia do Bordeira ☎ 282 973 119. Mon & Wed–Sun noon–10pm. Closed Nov. Around 1km back from Praia do Bordeira towards Carrapateira, this restaurant offers superb, mid-priced organic and free-range Portuguese food from €10, with an outdoor terrace.

Tasca da Saskia

Odeceixe ☎ 919 433 367. Tues–Sun 9am–midnight; restricted opening in winter. On the edge of town on the beach road, this former club has been turned into an arty bar-restaurant with great breakfasts, pasta, pizza and veggie meals from around €8. The innovative open-plan interior and roof terrace are often used for theme nights, gigs and film shows.

O Zé

Monte Clérigo ☎ 282 998 621. Daily 9am–10pm. The best positioned of Monte Clérigo's café-restaurants, with decently priced snacks, drinks and full Portuguese meals. The tables out the back face the beach.

Essentials

Arrival

Faro's modern **international airport**, 6km west of the town centre, is very well served by year-round charter, schedule and low-cost airlines. The airport has various standard facilities – ATM machines, exchange bureau, shops, post office and a tourist office (daily 8.30am–11pm; ☎ 289 818 582). A number of car rental companies also have offices at the airport. Most use a special car park right opposite the terminal, though some use a less convenient dropping-off point five minutes away; check with the company when you collect your car (see "Directory" for details).

For onward travel by public transport to other parts of the Algarve you'll need to make the short journey to Faro's central bus or train stations. Buses #14 and #16 run from the airport via both stations, which are a few minutes away from each other. The 20- to 25-minute ride costs €1.50 (7.10am–9pm, 8pm at weekends, roughly every 45min). Taxis to Faro take ten to fifteen minutes and should cost about €10; there's a twenty-percent surcharge between 10pm and 6am and at weekends. For details of train and bus travel, see below.

Transport

Trains are the least expensive form of public transport, though are rather on the slow side. The Algarve rail line runs from Lagos to Vila Real de Santo António on the Spanish border, linking with the Lisbon line (for connections to the continent) at Tunes. Going from west to east, you may have to change at Tunes, Faro or Tavira, depending on your destination. Free train timetables for the Algarve line are available from information desks at main stations. For national routes and fares, check ⓦ www .cp.pt or ☎ 808 208 208/289 803 090. Always turn up at the station with time to spare, as long queues often form at the ticket desk, though some smaller regional stations are sometimes unmanned, in which case just hop on and pay the ticket inspector on board. Children under 4 go free; under-12s pay half price. Senior citizens (over-65s) can get thirty percent off travel if they produce their passport (or other form of ID proving their age) and ask for a *Bilhete terceira idade*. Lastly, note that some train stations are quite far from the town or village they serve

and there's no guarantee of connecting transport.

It's almost always quicker to go by **bus** than by rail, if you can, though you'll pay slightly more. The main regional bus company is EVA (routes and timetables on ⓦ www.eva-transportes.pt, ☎ 289 899 760). Comfortable express buses operate on longer routes, including to Seville and Spain, for which you'll usually have to reserve tickets in advance. For other destinations in Portugal, the main carrier is Rede Expressos (fares and routes on ⓦ www.rede-expressos.pt).

Local bus stations (detailed in the text) are the place to pick up timetables and reserve seats. Note that services are considerably less frequent and occasionally non-existent at weekends.

Car rental and taxis

Car rental rates are among the lowest in Europe, but petrol (*gasolina*) is on a par with northern Europe. Most rental cars run on unleaded (*sem chumbo*), and some on diesel (*gasoil*). Driving licences from EU countries are accepted, otherwise an international driving licence is required. In large towns there are usually car parks where you pay by the hour, along with pay-and-display parking bays, for which you'll need exact change, although spaces are often at a premium in high season. You're also likely to come across enterprising locals pointing you to empty spaces; it's best to tip (around €0.50) for this service.

Traffic drives on the right: speed limits are 50kph in towns and villages; 90kph on normal roads; and 120kph on the motorways. At road junctions, unless there's a sign to the contrary, vehicles coming from the right have priority. Seat-belts are compulsory and children under 1.50m in height must use a booster seat. If you're stopped by the police, they'll want to see your documents – carry them in the car at all times. In the event of a breakdown, you must wear a col-oured sash (which will be provided by the car-hire company) when you leave the vehicle. Don't leave anything of value in an unattended car. See p.187 for a list of car hire companies.

Travelling by **taxi** in Portugal is rela-tively cheap and is worth considering for trips across major towns and for shorter journeys in rural areas. Generally, taxis are metered, with a minimum fare of €1.80. Additional charges are made for carrying baggage in the boot and for travelling between 10pm and 6am and at weekends. Outside major towns, you can negotiate if you want to hire a taxi for a few hours.

Bikes and mopeds

The Algarve is increasingly geared up to cyclists. A 214-kilometre trans-Algarve cycle-route – run by Ecovias (Ⓦ www .ecoviasalgarve.org) – now links Cabo de São Vicente in the west with Vila Real in the east. Bicycles are a great way of seeing the region, though pedalling can be hard work as pretty much everywhere inland, apart from the Rio Guadiana area, is hilly. Several specialist shops, hotels, campsites and youth hostels rent out bikes for around €10–15 a day, while organized bike tours (mostly off-road) are offered by The Mountain Bike Adventure (Ⓦ www.TheMountainBikeAdventure. com), mainly in the Lagos region. You can also rent mopeds, scooters and low-powered (80cc) motorbikes in many of the resorts, starting at around €30 a day. You need to be at least 18 (and over 23 to rent larger bikes over 125cc) and to have held a full licence for at least a year. Rental usually includes helmet hire and locks, along with third-party insurance.

Money

Despite being the most expensive region in Portugal, the Algarve remains notably cheaper than northern Europe and North America. Portugal is one of the twelve European Union countries to use the euro. Euro notes are issued in denominations of 5, 10, 20, 50, 100, 200 and 500 euro, and coins in denominations of 1, 2, 5, 10, 20 and 50 cents and 1 and 2 euro.

You'll find a **bank** in all but the small-est towns, and many have automatic exchange facilities. Standard opening hours are Monday to Friday 8.30am to 3pm. Changing cash in banks is easy and shouldn't attract more than €3 commission.

By far the easiest way to get money in Portugal is to use **ATMs** (called *Multi-banco*). You'll find them in even the most out-of-the-way small towns, and you can withdraw up to €200 per day. Check with your bank to see whether you can use your credit or debit card in the Algarve, and remember that on credit card withdrawals you'll be charged inter-est from day one in addition to the usual currency conversion fee, while debit cards can also incur per-transaction fees. Most Portuguese banks will give cash advances on cards over the counter, charging a currency conversion fee. Credit cards are also accepted in many hotels and restaurants.

Banks in Portugal charge an outrageous commission for changing **travellers' cheques** (upwards of €15 per transaction). However, more reasonable fees can be had in *caixas* – savings banks or building societies – and some exchange bureaux that often open in the evening. Larger hotels are sometimes willing to change travellers' cheques at low commission (though often at poor conversion rates). It's worth taking a supply in case your plastic is lost, stolen or swallowed by an ATM.

Accommodation

Most accommodation in the Algarve is fairly modern and there is a wide range to choose from. If you're travelling in high season (June to early Sept) you should try to reserve in advance.

Rooms and guesthouses

Some of the cheapest accommodation consists of **rooms** (*quartos* or *dormidas*) let out in private houses. These are sometimes advertised, or more often hawked at bus and train stations, and they can be good value. The local turismo may also have a list of rooms available. It's always worth haggling, and check the room is not too far from the centre. If you're not paying in advance, get the owner to write down the agreed price for you.

The main budget travel standby is a room in a **pensão** – officially graded from one to three stars (often, it seems, in a quite random fashion). Better ones usually have TVs and en-suite facilities. Many serve meals, but they rarely insist that you take them. *Pensões* that don't serve meals are sometimes called *residenciais* (singular *residencial* or *residência*). Similar to *pensões*, and generally at the cheaper end of the scale, are *hospedarias* or *casas de hóspedes* – boarding houses – which can be characterful places.

Hotels, inns and pousadas

A one-star **hotel** usually costs about the same as a three-star *pensão*, and is often similar in standard. Prices for two- and three-star hotels, though, see a notable shift upwards, with facilities such as a bar, restaurant or pool.

Rates for the four- and five-star hotel league are closer to those in northern Europe, with facilities to match, such as gyms, babysitting services and children's clubs. Similar to four- and five-star hotels are **inns**, called *estalagems* or *albergarias*.

Pousadas (literally "resting places") are part government-owned hotels, usually in historic buildings or castles. The Algarve has three characterful *pousadas*, reviewed in the text (p.74, p.88 and p.168), with a fourth in the pipeline; details on Ⓦ www.pousadas.pt.

Villas, apartments and youth hostels

Virtually every area of the Algarve has some sort of **villa** or **apartment** available for hire, from simple one-room apartments to luxurious five- or six-bed houses complete with garden and swimming pool. High summer sees the best places booked up months in advance (holiday and tour operators are useful if you want to book ahead). Expect to pay at least €70 a night in high season for an apartment for two people, up to €150 for a top villa, though one-week lets are usually the minimum. Outside peak period you should be able to turn up and bag somewhere for around 25 percent less, and 50 percent less in winter.

There are four **youth hostels** (*pousadas de juventude*) in the Algarve, most open all year round. Details are in the text, or see Ⓦ www.pousadasjuventude.pt.

Campsites

The Algarve has a number of authorized **campsites**, many in very attractive locations and, despite their often large size (over 500 spaces is not uncommon),

extremely crowded in summer. Most of the campsites have spaces for campervans and caravans and many also have permanent caravans and bungalows for rent. Charges are per person and per caravan or tent, with showers and parking extra; even so, it's rare that you'll end up paying more than €5 a person, although those operated by the Orbitur chain (Ⓦ www.orbitur.pt) are usually a little more expensive. Sites are detailed in the text, or see Ⓦ www.roteiro-campista.pt.

Camping outside official grounds is not allowed in the Algarve, though you'll rarely have problems parking a campervan behind some of the best, out-of-the-way beaches. Be warned, too, that thefts from campsites are a regular occurrence.

Information

You can pick up free brochures and maps from the Portuguese tourist office in your home country. Once in Portugal, get hold of a copy of the excellent *Turismo do Algarve Guide*, a monthly listings magazine in English and Portuguese, available free from most tourist offices and hotels.

You'll find a **turismo** (tourist office) in almost every town and village; details are given in the text. The offices are usually helpful and friendly, and English is spoken, though note that opening times tend to be fluid, depending on the availability of staff. There's also an excellent freephone line, Linha Verde Turista ☎ 808 781 212 (Mon–Fri 8am–7pm); the operators speak English and have information on museums, transport, accommodation, restaurants, hospitals and police stations.

The Portuguese National Tourist Office and turismos can provide you with a reasonable **map** of the country (1:600,000), which is fine for everything except mountain roads. If you're doing any real exploration, however, it's worth investing in a good road map such as

the *Rough Guide Map: The Algarve* (1:100,000).

Most resorts sell international **newspapers** – often the previous day's. *The News* (Ⓦ www.the-news.net) is an English-language weekly national, while the *Algarve Resident* is a weekly covering local news and events.

Useful websites

Ⓦ **www.algarvenet.com** Detailed site dedicated to the Algarve, covering everything from tourist sites to weather and shopping.

Ⓦ **www.maisturismo.pt** Search engine for hotels, mostly business-oriented or at the top end of the market.

Ⓦ **www.portugal.org** Government-run tourist site, with an Algarve section.

Ⓦ **www.Portugal-info.net** Links to various sites covering everything from accommodation and flights to sports and wine.

Ⓦ **www.portugalvirtual.pt** Links with extensive hotel and villa listings, restaurants and bars, as well as shops and transport.

Ⓦ **www.visitalgarve.pt** The official tourist board site. Information is thorough.

Food and drink

Portuguese food tends to be inexpensive and served in big portions, and even the humblest bar can serve one of Portugal's excellent local wines. At their finest, dishes can be superb, made with fresh ingredients bursting with flavour. Grilled meats and fish tend to be the best bets, usually accompanied by chips, rice or boiled potatoes and salad. But don't expect sophisticated sauces or delicate touches: stews, in particular, are not for the faint-hearted; offal features highly on many menus and even the ever-present *bacalhau* (salted dried cod) can be heavy going: you're probably best off going for *bacalhau à bras* (with egg, potatoes and onion) or *com natas* (with a creamy sauce). For all that though, Portuguese **restaurants** tend to be very good value. It's always worth checking the *ementa turística* – a three-course set meal, including a drink – and the *prato do dia* (dish of the day), which often features a local speciality. As well as restaurants, you'll come across *tascas* (small taverns), *casas de pasto* (inexpensive diners, often lunches only) and *churrascarias* (specializing in grilled meat and fish). *Cervejarias* are literally a "beer houses", more informal than a restaurant and offering drinks and snacks as well as full meals. Finally, *marisqueiras* have a superior fish- and seafood-based menu. You'll also find no shortage of international restaurants in the Algarve.

Most restaurants are **open** noon–3pm for lunch and 7.30–11pm for dinner. All places have a cover charge for bread, but remember that any other starters put on your table will be charged for – tell the waiter if you do not want them.

In this guide, we have rated a two-course meal with a drink as inexpensive for under €15, mid-priced at €15–25, and expensive at over €25.

There is little to distinguish many **cafés and bars** in Portugal, and most sell both coffee and alcohol throughout the day. *Pastelarias* specialize in pastries and cakes (*bolos*) and are also good stops for breakfast croissants and breads. For light lunches, cafés and bars do snacks that usually include *rissóis de carne* (meat patties), *pastéis de bacalhau/carne/camerão* (salted cod/meat/shrimp rissoles), *chouriço* (smoked sausage) and *sandes de queijo/fiambre* (cheese or ham sandwiches). Coffee is invariably fresh and of good quality. *Uma bica* is a strong espresso, *um galão* is a weak milky coffee in a tall glass, while *uma café com leite* is a normal coffee with milk. Children are welcome in most bars, where you can buy soft drinks as well as inexpensive local drinks such as Sagres or Super Bock beer and gigantic measures of spirits. Local firewaters include *medronho*, made from the fruit of the strawberry tree, *Algarviana*, made from almonds, and *brandymel*, a honey brandy.

Festivals and events

The Ministry of Culture's website, ⓦ www .min-cultura.pt/Agenda/Agenda.jsp, can give more details on many of the events and festivals listed below.

January

Lisbon-Daka Rally A leg of the gruelling rally races through the Algarve during January.

February

Carnival Loulé has one of the best of the region's lively carnival parades, with costumed processions through town.

March/April

Aleluia procession, Easter Sunday São Brás de Alportel has the most distinctive of the region's various Easter processions.

Mãe Soberana, Loulé The Algarve's biggest religious festival begins when the image of Our Lady of Piety is carried from the hilltop church of Nossa Senhora da Piedade to the Church of São Francisco on Easter Sunday before being returned two weeks later in a solemn procession.

May 1

Atacar o Maio Literally "attacking May", when May 1 is celebrated with dried figs and *medronho* brandy accompanied by folk music. In Monchique, *medronho* is drunk and *mel* (honey) is eaten with *Bolo do Tacho* – pot cake made from corn flour, honey and chocolate. In Estoi, pine cones and rosemary are laid at the church of Our Lady of Pé da Cruz, with an evening torchlit procession and fireworks.

Alte Week of Arts and Culture Live shows, brass bands and folk dancing are accompanied by a grand picnic in May.

Algarve International Cinema Festival Cinemas in Portimão, Alvor and Praia da Rocha screen films from both Portuguese and international directors throughout May.

June

Algarve International Music Festival The biggest cultural event in the Algarve, organized by the Gulbenkian Foundation and others, with chamber music, ballet and top

Food festivals

January

Smoked Sausage Fair, Querença. Somewhat ironically celebrates Saint Luís, the patron saint of animals.

March

Smoked Sausage Fair, Monchique. Local produce market and special menus in restaurants, along with live music.

May

Gastronomy Festival, Portimão. Restaurants serve typically Portuguese dishes from various regions.

June

Week of Portuguese Gastronomy, Lagoa. Gourmets prepare the best of Portuguese food, plus a handicrafts fair.

Cataplana Festival, Almancil. Restaurants in the region make dishes using the traditional *cataplana* pressure cooker.

July

Beer Festival, Silves. Held in the Fábrica Inglês, with beers from around the world.

Sweet Fair, Lagos. Sculpted egg, almond and fig sweets are sold along with other local produce.

Presunto Festival, Monchique. The place to try cured hams, in the town famed for them.

August

Festival do Marisco, Olhão. Fish and seafood festival with live music.

Sardine Festival, Quarteira. An enormous grill on the beach cooks several hundred kilos of fish.

Petiscos Festival, Querença. Small tapas-like dishes are served accompanied by dancing and music.

September

Sweet potato and barnacle festival, Aljezur. The west coast town shows off its local specialities and puts on live entertainment.

November

Chestnut festival, Marmelete, Alferce and Vale Silves. More fresh food and revelry accompany the autumn harvests.

international artists performing at venues throughout the region; runs until August.

Algarve Summer Festival A weekend of top musical acts sells out the 30,000 capacity Algarve Stadium; Black Eyed Peas and James Blunt have appeared in previous years.

Festa de Santo António (June 12–13) A celebration of one of the most important of the popular saints, with music, food, drink and all-night dancing in Faro, Tavira, Quarteira and smaller towns.

Festa de São João (June 23–24) Processions and music throughout the region – especially Lagoa, Lagos, Monchique and Portimão – celebrating the feast day of São João (Saint John).

Festa de São Pedro (June 28–29) St Peter's day is celebrated with revelry until the small hours.

July

Loulé International Jazz Festival Local and international jazz performers play at weekends throughout July.

Feira do Carmo, Faro The town's big annual fair, with handicrafts and live entertainment. Also celebrated with a parade of boats at Fuzeta.

International Motorcycle Concentration Annual leather-clad celebration with rock bands playing between Faro beach and Faro airport.

August–September

Medieval Fair. Jugglers, acrobats and markets recreate medieval life in Silves.

Fatacil, Lagoa Big agricultural trade fair in mid-August with displays of local goods backed by music and entertainment.

Coimbra Serenades Top Coimbra Fado – the distinctly Portuguese version of the blues – is performed throughout the region in August.

Medieval Days, Castro Marim Recreations of medieval jousts and pageants, usually late August.

Espectáculos de Folclore Folk performances around the Algarve in August and September with a grand finale on Portimão's waterfront.

October

Feira de Santa Iria, Largo de São Francisco, Faro Second of the big Faro fairs, with a week of craft stalls, bumper cars, music and daily festivities in October.

October–November

Autumn Fairs Stalls sell food and handicrafts at markets throughout the region in October and November.

São Martinho (November 11) Saint's day celebrated by eating roasted chestnuts – especially round the mountain village of Monchique – and drinking *agua pé* ("foot water"), the first tasting of this year's wine harvest.

December 24

Christmas Eve Christmas Eve is the main Christmas celebration, with a traditional *bacalhau* supper after midnight Mass.

December 31

New Year's Eve Enthusiastic banging of pots and pans heralds the new year, with live entertainment and fireworks throughout the region.

The Algarve's golf courses

Portugal's year-round mild climate and top facilities make it ideal for golf. Unsurprisingly, the Algarve's courses are not cheap, with green fees at up to €150 for eighteen holes. The best way to guarantee a round is to go on a special golf-holiday package (try Ⓦ www .playgolfinportugal.com) or to stay at one of the hotels or villas attached to golf clubs, which usually charge guests discounted rates (of up to fifty percent). For more information, see the excellent website Ⓦ www.algarvegolf.net. The following is a round-up of the main courses, listed according to the nearest main town or resort.

Albufeira
Pine Cliffs Praia da Falésia ☎289 500 113, ⓔgolf.Algarve@starwoodhotels.com. No handicap certificate required.
Salgados ☎289 583 030, ⓔgeral @salgadagolf.com. No handicap certificate required.

Alvor
Alto Golf Quinta do Alto do Poço ☎282 410 820, ⓔgolf@altogolf.com. Handicap max 28 men; 36 women.
Penina Golf Club, Penina ☎282 420 200, ⓔgolf.penina@starwoodhotels.com. Handicap max 28 men; 36 women.

Carvoeiro
Gramacho ☎282 340 900, ⓔinfo @pestanagolf.com. No handicap certificate required.
Vale de Milho ☎282 358 502, ⓔvaledemilhgolf@mail.telepac.pt. No handicap certificate required.
Vale de Pinta ☎282 340 900, ⓕinfo @pestanagolf.com. Handicap max 27 men; 35 women.

Castro Marim
Castro Marim Golf ☎281 510 330, ⓔgolf@castromarimgolfe/com. No handicap certificate required.

Lagos
Boavista ☎282 782 151, ⓔgolf .reception@boavistagolf.com. No handicap certificate required.

Manta Rota/Altura
Quinta da Ria/Quinta de Cima Vila Nova de Cacela ☎281 950 580, ⓔinfo @quintadaria.com. No handicap certificate required.

Meia Praia
Palmares ☎282 790 500, ⓔgolf @palmaresgolf.com. Handicap max 28 men; 36 women.

Quarteira
Vila Sol Morgadinhos Alto de Semino, Quarteira/Vilamoura ☎289 300 522, ⓔgolfreservations@vilasol.pt. Handicap max 24 men; 35 women.

Quinta do Lago
São Lorenço ☎289 396 908, ⓔsan.Lorenzo@lemeridien-algarve.com. Handicap max 28 men; 36 women.
Quinta do Lago/Ria Formosa ☎289 390 700, ⓔgeral@quintadolagogolf.com. Handicap max 26 men; 35 women.
Pinheiros Altos ☎289 359 910, ⓕ289 394 392. Handicap max 28 men; 36 women.

Salema
Parque da Floresta Vale do Poço ☎282 690 054, ⓔgolf@vigiasa.com. No handicap certificate required.

Tavira
Benamor Quinta de Benamor ☎281 320 880, ⓔreservas@golfbenamor.com. Handicap max 28 men; 36 women.

Vale de Lobo
Vale do Lobo ☎289 353 535, ⓔgolf @vdl.pt. Handicap max 28 men (Ocean Course), 27 (Royal Course), 36 women (Ocean Course), 35 (Royal Course).

Vilamoura
Laguna (Vilamoura III) ☎289 310 180, ⓔreservas-golfe@vilamouragolf.com. Handicap 28 men; 36 women.
Millennium ☎289 310 188, ⓕ289 310 183. Handicap 24 men; 28 women.
The Old Course (Vilamoura I) ☎289 310 341, ⓔreservas-golfe@vilamouragolf.com. Handicap max 24 men; 28 women.
Pinhal (Vilamoura II) ☎289 310 390, ⓕ289 310 393. Handicap 28 men; 36 women.
Victoria ☎289 320 100, ⓔvictoriagolf @vilamouragolf.com. Handicap 24 men; 28 women.

Directory

Addresses Addresses are written with the name of the road first followed by the number. The numbers 1°, 2° etc mean first, second floor etc. The ground floor (first floor in US) is marked r/c (*rés-do-chão*). You may also see d/dto or e/esq after the number, which mean on the right (*direito*) or left (*esquerda*) of the main staircase.
Airlines British Airways (☎218 445 353, ⓦwww.british-airways.com); Portugália (Lisbon ☎218 938 070, ⓦwww.flypga.com

/atrio); TAP Air Portugal, Rua Dom Francisco Gomes 8, Faro (℡289 800 200, ⓦwww .flytap.com).

Airport flight information ℡289 800 800.

Car hire companies AutoJardim (℡289 800 881, ⓦwww.auto-jardim.com); Avis (℡800 201 002, ⓦwww.avis .com.pt); Hertz (℡800 238 238, ⓦwww .hertz.com); Luzcar (also rents out motorbikes), Lagos (℡282 761 016, ⓦluzcar .com); Zitauto (℡289 315 559, ⓦwww .zitautorentacar.co.uk).

Children Most hotels and guesthouses can provide cots free of charge if given advance notice, and discounts are usually offered for children who share their parents' room. International-brand baby foods and nappies are widely available from supermarkets and chemists, though fresh milk (*leite do dia*) can usually only be bought from larger supermarkets. Some restaurants offer children's menus – alternatively, nearly all do half portions (*meia doce*). Take great care with the sun – children should be covered up or in the shade between 11am and 3pm.

Cinemas Most of the larger towns have cinemas, often inexpensive multiplexes showing the latest blockbusters. Films are shown in original language with Portuguese subtitles.

Consulates Canada, Rua Frei Lourenço Santa Maria 1–1º, Apt. 79, Faro (℡289 803 757); Denmark, Rua Conselheiro Bívar 10–1º, Faro (℡289 805 561); Netherlands, Largo Francisco Sá Carneiro 52, Faro (℡289 820 903); UK, Largo Francisco A. Maurício 7–1º, Apt. 609, Portimão (℡282 490 750). Most countries also have embassies in Lisbon.

Disabled access Portuguese people will go out of their way to make your visit as straightforward as possible, though special facilities remain limited. There are adapted WCs and wheelchair facilities at the airport and reserved disabled parking spaces in main cities, where the Orange Badge is recognized. National tourist offices can supply a list of wheelchair-accessible hotels and campsites; some are listed in the text, or contact Wheeling Around the Algarve (℡289 393 636, ⓦwww .player.pt), which organizes holiday accommodation, transport and sporting/ leisure activities.

Electricity Portugal uses two-pin plugs (220v). UK appliances will work with a continental adaptor.

Emergencies ℡112 for fire, police and ambulance (free).

Football The Algarve is not the traditional hotbed of Portuguese soccer, though Portimonense from Portimão have had spells in the top division. Top international games are sometimes held at the Algarve stadium (see p.56). The season runs from September to May. For details of fixtures, see ⓦwww.portuguese.soccer.com, or buy the daily sports paper, *A Bola*.

Gay travellers Though traditionally a conservative and macho society, Portugal has become increasingly tolerant of homosexuality. The Lisbon-based Centro Comunitário Gay e Lesbica de Lisboa (℡218 873 918, Wed–Sat 6pm–midnight) publishes gay listings on ⓦwww.ilga-portugal.pt rg. Reader-vote listings can also be found on ⓦwww .portugalgay.pt, though the information – in Portuguese – is not updated regularly.

Hospitals Hospital Distrital de Faro, Leão Penedo, Faro ℡289 891 100; Hospital Distrital, Rua do Castelo dos Governadores, Lagos ℡282 700 100; Hospital do Barlavento Algarvio, Sítio do Poço Seco, Portimão ℡282 450 330. There are also various private clinics; get details from the local tourist office.

Internet and mail Post offices (*correios*) are normally open Mon–Fri 9am–6pm. Nearly all post offices contain terminals for Internet access, for which prepaid cards can be bought at the counter. Stamps (*selos*) are sold at post offices, from automatic machines on streets and anywhere that has the sign "Correio de Portugal – Selos" displayed.

Opening times Official opening times are given in the text, but note that for many cafés, shops, restaurants and tourist offices, opening times are not rigidly adhered to. This is especially so in smaller places and out of season, when places may open late or not at all in bad weather or during quiet periods. Typical shopping hours are Monday to Friday, 9am–1pm & 2.30/3–7/8pm and Saturday 9am–1pm. Larger supermarkets and many resort shops open daily, often until 11pm.

Pharmacies Pharmacies are open Mon–Fri 9am–1pm & 3–7pm, Sat 9am–1pm. Local papers carry information about 24hr pharmacies, and the details are posted on every pharmacy door.

Public holidays Official holidays are: January 1 (New Year's Day); February/ March (Carnival); Good Friday; April 25 (celebrating the 1974 revolution); May 1 (Labour Day); June 10 (Portugal Day and Camões Day); August 15 (Feast of the Assumption); October 5 (Republic Day);

Fly Less – Stay Longer!

Rough Guides believes in the good that travel does, but we are deeply aware of the impact of fuel emissions on climate change. We recommend taking fewer trips and staying for longer. If you can avoid travelling by air, please use an alternative, especially for journeys of under 1000km/600miles. And always offset your travel at ⓦ www.roughguides.com/climatechange.

November 1 (All Saints' Day); December 1 (Independence Day, celebrating independence from Spain in 1640); December 8 (Immaculate Conception); December 24–25 (Christmas).

Sunbathing Portugal can be traditional and formal: topless bathing is rare on town beaches, though nudism is common on more out-of-the-way beaches.

Time Portugal is in the same time zone as the UK: GMT (late Oct to late March) and BST (late March to late Oct). This is five hours ahead of Eastern Standard Time and eight hours ahead of Pacific Standard Time.

Tipping Service charges are normally included in hotel bills and in the larger restaurants. Smaller restaurants, cafés and bars do not expect a large tip; simply round up the change or leave ten percent of the bill.

Toilets There are very few public toilets. However, nearly all the main tourist sights have a public toilet (*casa de banho, retrete, banheiro, lavabos* or *WC*), and it is not difficult to sneak into a café or restaurant. Gents are usually marked H (*homens*) or C (*cabalheiros*), and ladies M (*mulheres*) or S (*senhoras*). Note that many older buildings – including hotels and villas – have very narrow drains, so to avoid blockages you are expected to put toilet paper in the bins provided, not down the loo.

Women will experience few problems travelling alone in the Algarve: they may attract some unwanted attention in the beach resorts, but it is unlikely to be insistent or threatening.

Chronology

Algarve chronology

500 BC ▶ Greeks and Carthaginians visit the Algarve to trade in salt and tuna paste – a popular commodity in classical Athens.

60 BC ▶ Most of what is now Portugal is integrated into the Roman Empire under Julius Caesar.

27 BC ▶ Emperor Augustus divides Roman Iberia into two provinces. Lusitania stretches from what is now the Algarve north to the Douro. Roman bridges are built at Silves (Silbis) and Tavira (Balsa).

2 AD ▶ Romans develop Milreu near Faro, the spa at Caldas de Monchique, salt extracting plants at modern day Quinta da Marim and the Cerra da Vila complex at Vilamoura.

585 ▶ Christian Visigoths take over Iberia and establish their capital in Toledo. A bishopric is established at Faro.

711 ▶ Originally invited to help out a faction of squabbling Visigoths, the first wave of Moors crosses into Spain. Within a decade, they have taken over most of Iberia.

9th century ▶ The Moors establish the independent kingdom of al-Gharb ("the west") with its capital at Shelb (Silves). Roman irrigation techniques are improved as the Moors introduce the cultivation of citrus fruits and almonds and crafts such as *azulejos* tiles.

1073 ▶ Portucale is given country status by the kings of León in the area between the Douro and Minho rivers.

12th century ▶ Portuguese monarchs, backed by Christian crusaders, expand their kingdom south, taking Lisbon from the Moors in 1147.

1249 ▶ After several temporary victories and counter-attacks, Afonso III finally takes Faro from the Moors to establish a united Portugal. Monarchs are crowned "king/queen of Portugal and the Algarve" until the republic is established in 1910.

1279–1325 ▶ Dom Dinis protects his borders with a string of castles. Much of the sparsely populated Algarve is entrusted to noblemen, the Church and holy orders – notably the Order of Christ, who establish their base at Castro Marim.

1386 ▶ The Treaty of Windsor seals a trading alliance with England. Portugal's new commercial clout encourages Castile to cease ongoing hostilities, allowing Portugal to prosper.

15th century ▶ Overseas explorations depart from Lagos and Portimão, bringing back spices, precious metals, gold – and slaves. Many pioneering farmers leave the Algarve to settle in Portugal's new-found colonies in Madeira and the Azores.

1420–1434 ▶ Henry the Navigator establishes a school of navigation at Sagres, redesigning the caravel and training the leading cartographers and mariners of the age. Lagos-born Gil Eanes sails round Cape Bojador in 1434 – then believed to be the edge of the world.

1487–1500 ▶ Bartolomeu Dias, a knight of the Order of Christ, sets off from Portimão and becomes the first European to sail round the southern tip of Africa. He then joins Vasco da Gama on his historic journey to India in 1498, and Pedro Alvares Cabral, who "discovers" Brazil in 1500.

16th century ▶ Portugal, along with Spain, dominate world trade, with strategic trading posts established in Goa (1510), Malacca (1511), Ormuz (1515) and Macau (1517).

1577 ▶ An important port and centre for slave traders, Lagos becomes capital of the Algarve.

1578 ▶ After rousing his troops in Lagos, Dom Sebastião suffers a crushing defeat at the battle of Alcácer-Quibrir in a failed crusade in Morocco. Much of Portugal's nobility is wiped out.

1580–1640 ▶ Cardinal Henrique dies without an heir, and after victory at the battle of Alcântara, Philip II of Spain becomes Felipe I of Portugal.

1587 ▶ Now under Spanish rule, Portugal becomes a target for the British, and Sir Francis Drake sacks Lagos and Sagres.

1640 ▶ A group of conspirators storm the palace in Lisbon and establish the Bragança family as Portugal's new monarchs. Spain officially recognizes Portuguese independence in 1668.

1755–1776 ▶ The Great Earthquake flattens Lisbon and much of the Algarve. The provincial capital is moved from ravaged Lagos to Faro in 1776.

1807–1811 ▶ Napoleon's troops march into Lisbon and Portugal's royal family flee to Brazil. Algarve resistance fighters force out the occupying forces briefly in 1808, but it is not until 1811 that Wellington and Beresford repel Napoleon's army.

19th century ▶ Industrialization sees the opening of a new Lisbon–Faro railway in 1889, though most of the region relies on fish canning, cork and agriculture.

1910 ▶ Manuel II is exiled, as the army and navy overthrow the monarchy, establishing the republic.

1928–1968 ▶ Dr António de Oliveira Salazar rules the country with an iron fist. Although a relatively modern economy emerges, rural areas such as the Algarve are left to stagnate.

1965 ▶ The need for foreign income persuades Salazar to open up the Algarve to tourists. Modern hotels appear and an airport opens at Faro.

1974 ▶ Popular resentment of the inward-looking regime ushers in a largely peaceful revolution. Many colonialists return to Portugal and set up tourist businesses. The Algarve grows more popular as a destination.

1986 ▶ Portugal's entry to the European Community ushers in a massive injection of funds. The Algarve's infrastructure improves and a rash of tourist developments begins.

1990–2003 ▶ A new east-west highway and bridge over to Spain opens up the Algarve even more, though the establishment of the Parque Natural do Costa Vicentina in 1995 protects a swathe of the district from development.

2004– ▶ The Algarve Stadium is built to host the European Football Championships. Planning permission is granted for up to 50 golf courses in the region.

Language

Language

English is widely spoken throughout the Algarve, but you will find a few words of Portuguese extremely useful if you are travelling on public transport or in more out-of-the-way places. If you have some knowledge of Spanish, you won't have much problem reading Portuguese. Understanding it when it's spoken, though, is a different matter: pronunciation is entirely different and at first even the easiest words are hard to distinguish.

A useful word is *há* (the H is silent), which means "there is" or "is there?" and can be used for just about anything. Thus: "*Há uma pensão aqui?*" ("Is there a pension here?"). More polite and better in shops or restaurants are "*Tem…?*" (pronounced *taying*) which means "Do you have…?", or "*Queria…*" ("I'd like…"). And of course there are the old standards "Do you speak English?" (*Fala Inglês?*) and "I don't understand" (*Não compreendo*).

Pronunciation

The chief difficulty with pronunciation is its lack of clarity – consonants tend to be slurred, vowels nasal and often ignored altogether. The **consonants** are, at least, consistent:

C is soft before E and I, hard otherwise unless it has a cedilla – *açucar* (sugar) is pronounced "assookar".

CH is somewhat softer than in English; *chá* (tea) sounds like Shah.

J is pronounced like the "s" in pleasure, as is G except when it comes before a "hard" vowel (A, O and U).

LH sounds like "lyuh" (Alcantarilha).

Q is always pronounced as a "k".

S before a consonant or at the end of a word becomes "sh," otherwise it's as in English – Sagres is pronounced "Sahgresh".

X is also pronounced "sh" – *caixa* (cash desk) is pronounced "kaisha".

Vowels are worse – flat and truncated, they're often difficult for English-speaking tongues to get around. The only way to learn is to listen: accents, **Ã**, **Ô**, or **É**, turn them into longer, more familiar sounds.

When two vowels come together they continue to be enunciated separately except in the case of **El** and **OU** – which sound like "a" and long "o" respectively. E at the end of a word is silent unless it has an accent, so that *carne* (meat) is pronounced "karn", while *café* sounds much as you'd expect. The **tilde over Ã or Õ** renders the pronunciation much like the French -an and -on endings, only more nasal. More common is **ÃO** (as in *pão*, bread – *são*, saint – *limão*, lemon), which sounds something like a strangled yelp of "Ow!" cut off in midstream.

Words and phrases

LANGUAGE

Basics

sim; não	yes; no
olá; bom dia	hello; good morning
boa tarde/noite	good afternoon/ night
adeus, até logo	goodbye, see you later
hoje; amanhã	today; tomorrow
por favor/se faz favor	please
tudo bem?	everything all right?
está bem	it's all right/OK
obrigado/a*	thank you
onde; que	where; what
quando; porquê	when; why
como; quanto	how; how much
não sei	I don't know
sabe . . .?	do you know . . .?
pode . . .?	could you . . .?
desculpe; com licença	sorry; excuse me
este/a; esse/a	this; that
agora; mais tarde	now; later
mais; menos	more; less
grande; pequeno	big; little
aberto; fechado	open; closed
senhoras; homens	women; men
lavabo/quarto de banho	toilet/bathroom
turismo	tourist office
praia	beach
igreja	church
jardim	garden
mercado	market
museu	museum
parque	park
praça/largo	square
sé	cathedral

*Obrigado agrees with the sex of the person speaking – a woman says obrigada, a man obrigado.

Getting around

esquerda, direita, sempre em frente	left, right, straight ahead
aqui; ali	here; there
perto; longe	near; far
Onde é a estação de camionetas?	Where is the bus station?
a paragem de autocarro para...	the bus stop for . .
Donde parte o autocarro para...?	Where does the bus to . . . leave from?
A que horas parte?	What time does it leave?
(chega a . . .?)	(arrive at . . .?)
Pare aqui por favor	Stop here please
bilhete (para)	ticket (to)
ida e volta	round trip

Accommodation

Queria um quarto	I'd like a room
É para uma noite (semana)	It's for one night (week)
É para uma pessoa	It's for one person
(duas pessoas)	two people
Quanto custa?	How much is it?
Posso ver?	May I see/ look around?
Há um quarto mais barato?	Is there a cheaper room?
com duche	with a shower
pousada	Inn
pousada de juventude	Youth hostel

Shopping

Quanto é?	How much is it?
banco; câmbio	bank; change
correios	post office
(dois) selos	(two) stamps
Como se diz isto em Português?	What's this called in Portuguese?
O que é isso?	What's that?
artesenato	craft shop
farmácia	chemist

Common Portuguese signs

Aberto	open
Desvio	diversion (on road)
Dormidas	private rooms for rent
Elevador	lift
Entrada	entrance
Fecha a porta	close the door
Fechado	closed
Obras	road or building works
Perigo/Perigoso	danger/dangerous
Paragem	bus stop

Pré-pagamento	pay in advance
Proibido estacionar	no parking
Saída	exit

Days of the week

domingo	Sunday
segunda-feira	Monday
terça-feira	Tuesday
quarta-feira	Wednesday
quinta-feira	Thursday
sexta-feira	Friday
sábado	Saturday

Numbers

1	um
2	dois
3	três
4	quatro
5	cinco
6	seis
7	sete
8	oito
9	nove
10	dez
11	onze
12	doze
13	treze
14	catorze
15	quinze
16	dezasseis
17	dezassete
18	dezoito
19	dezanove
20	vinte
21	vinte e um
30	trinta
40	quarenta
50	cinquenta
60	sessenta
70	setenta
80	oitenta
90	noventa
100	cem
101	cento e um
200	duzentos
500	quinhentos
1000	mil

Food and drink

Places to eat and drink

adega	literally a wine cellar; also does food
casa de pasto	a lunchtime diner
cervejaria	a beer hall, also does food
churrasqueria	a grill house
marisqueira	restaurant specializing in fish and seafood
pastelaria	a patisserie
taberna	a tavern

Basic words and terms

almoço	lunch
assado	roasted
colher	spoon
conta	bill
copo	glass
cozido	boiled
ementa	menu
estrelado/frito	fried
faca	knife
fumado	smoked
garfo	fork
garrafa	bottle
grelhado	grilled
jantar	dinner
mexido	scrambled
pastéis de nata	flaky custard tartlets
pequeno almoço	breakfast
petiscos	tapas-like snacks

Soups, salad and staples

arroz	rice
azeitonas	olives
batatas fritas	chips/french fries
caldo verde	cabbage soup
fruta	fruit
gaspacho	chilled vegetable soup
legumes	vegetables
manteiga	butter
ovos	eggs
pão	bread

pimenta	pepper
piri-piri	chilli sauce
queijo	cheese
sal	salt
salada	salad
sopa de legumes	vegetable soup
sopa de marisco	shellfish soup
sopa de peixe	fish soup

Fish and shellfish

arroz de marisco	seafood rice
atum	tuna
bacalhau à brás	salted cod with egg and potatoes
besugo	red sea bream
caldeirada	fish stew
camarões	shrimp
carapau	mackerel
cataplana	fish, shellfish or meat stewed in a circular metal dish
cherne	stone bass
dourada	bream
espada	scabbard fish
espadarte	swordfish
feijoada	rich bean stew, with fish or meat
gambas	prawns
lagosta	lobster
lampreia	lamprey
lulas (grelhadas)	squid (grilled)
pescada	hake
polvo	octopus
mexilhões	mussels
robalo	sea bass
salmonete	red mullet
salmão	salmon
sapateira	crab
santola	spider crab
sardinhas na brasa	charcoal-grilled sardines
truta	trout
viera	scallop

Meat

bife à portuguesa	thin beef steak with a fried egg on top
borrego	lamb
chouriço	spicy sausage
coelho	rabbit
cozido à portuguesa	boiled casserole of meats and beans, served with rice and vegetables
dobrada	tripe
espetada mista	mixed meat kebab
fiambre	ham
febras	pork steaks
frango no churrasco	barbecued chicken
pato	duck
perdiz	partridge
perú	turkey
carne de porco à alentejana	pork cooked with clams
presunto	smoked ham
vitela	veal

Drinks

um copo/ uma garrafa de/da...	a glass/bottle of...
vinho branco/tinto	white/red wine
cerveja	beer
água (sem/com gás)	water (with/ without gas)
sumo de laranja/ maçã	orange/apple juice
chá/café	tea/coffee
sem/com leite	without/with milk
sem/com açúcar	without/with sugar
medronho	a schapps-like liqueur made from the fruit of the strawberry tree
vinho verde	young, slightly sparkling wine

small print & Index

SMALL PRINT

A Rough Guide to Rough Guides

In 1981, Mark Ellingham, a recent graduate in English from Bristol University, was travelling in Greece on a tiny budget and couldn't find the right guidebook. With a group of friends he wrote his own guide, combining a contemporary, journalistic style with a practical approach to travellers' needs. That first Rough Guide was a student scheme that became a publishing phenomenon. Today, Rough Guides include recommendations from shoestring to luxury and cover hundreds of destinations around the globe, including almost every country in the Americas and Europe, more than half of Africa and most of Asia and Australasia. Millions of readers relish Rough Guides' wit and inquisitiveness as much as their enthusiastic, critical approach and value-for-money ethos. The guides' ever-growing team of authors and photographers is spread all over the world.

In the early 1990s, Rough Guides branched out of travel, with the publication of Rough Guides to World Music, Classical Music and the Internet. All three have become benchmark titles in their fields, spearheading the publication of a range of more than 350 titles under the Rough Guide name, including phrasebooks, waterproof maps, music guides from Opera to Heavy Metal, reference works as diverse as Conspiracy Theories and Shakespeare, and popular culture books from iPods to Poker. Rough Guides also produce a series of more than 120 World Music CDs in partnership with World Music Network.

Visit www.roughguides.com to see our latest publications.

Rough Guide travel images are available for commercial licensing at www.roughguidespictures.com

Publishing information

This second edition published April 2008 by **Rough Guides Ltd**, 80 Strand, London WC2R 0RL. 345 Hudson St, 4th Floor, New York, NY 10014, USA.

Distributed by the Penguin Group
Penguin Books Ltd, 80 Strand, London WC2R 0RL
Penguin Group (USA), 375 Hudson Street, NY 10014, USA
14 Local Shopping Centre, Panchsheel Park, New Delhi 110017, India
Penguin Group (Australia), 250 Camberwell Road, Camberwell, Victoria 3124, Australia
Penguin Group (Canada), 10 Alcorn Avenue, Toronto, ON M4V 1E4, Canada
Penguin Group (NZ), 67 Apollo Drive, Mairangi Bay, Auckland 1310, New Zealand
Typeset in Bembo and Helvetica to an original design by Henry Iles.

Cover concept by Peter Dyer.

Printed and bound in China
© Matthew Hancock 2008

No part of this book may be reproduced in any form without permission from the publisher except for the quotation of brief passages in reviews.
208pp includes index

A catalogue record for this book is available from the British Library

ISBN 978-1-85828-000-4

The publishers and authors have done their best to ensure the accuracy and currency of all the information in **Algarve DIRECTIONS**, however, they can accept no responsibility for any loss, injury, or inconvenience sustained by any traveller as a result of information or advice contained in the guide.

1   3   5   7   9   8   6   4   2

Help us update

We've gone to a lot of effort to ensure that the second edition of Algarve DIRECTIONS is accurate and up-to-date. However, things change – places get "discovered", opening hours are notoriously fickle, restaurants and rooms raise prices or lower standards. If you feel we've got it wrong or left something out, we'd like to know, and if you can remember the address, the price, the phone number, so much the better.

Please send your comments with the subject line "Algarve DIRECTIONS Update" to ✉mail@roughguides.com. or by post to the above address We'll credit all contributions and send a copy of the next edition (or any other Rough Guide if you prefer) for the very best emails. Have your questions answered and tell others about your trip at ✪community.roughguides.com

Rough Guide credits

Text editor: Ruth Blackmore
Layout: Umesh Aggarwal
Photography: Eddie Gerald and Matthew Hancock
Cartography: Swati Handoo

Picture editor: Mark Thomas
Proofreader: Jan McCann
Production: Rebecca Short
Cover design: Chloë Roberts

SMALL PRINT

The author

Matthew Hancock fell in love with Portugal while working in Lisbon and later returned to the country to complete a 775-mile-long walk along the Spanish-Lisbon border. He is also author of *Lisbon DIRECTIONS* and *Madeira DIRECTIONS* and co-author of *The Rough Guide to Portugal*.

Acknowledgements

The author would like to thank Amanda Tomlin, Alex and Olivia for ideas and support; also Luisa Azevedo, Carlos Oliveira, José Arragão and Luís Pinto at ICEP; Natalie Jesus at the Algarve Tourist Board; and Julie Jarratt.

Readers' letters

Thanks to all the readers who took the time to write in with their comments and suggestions (and apologies to anyone whose name we've misspelt or omitted):

Maureen and Lorne Anton, Theresa Arnold and Teresa Pereira, Robert Asher, JH Aston, Garth Baker, J Beatson, Rosie Belcher, Richard Bennett, Asier Berra, Alan Bolister, Jonathan and Chris Chapman, Mary Cox and John Hopkins, Sandra Cunha, Beryl and Dave Frost, Susie Hargreaves, Victor and Hellena Gallant, H Greer, Mark Judd, Sadiq Kassamo, Mats Kullstedt and Eva Noble, Paulo Lopes, Terence Maguire, Muriel and Andr Mandi, Timothy Nodder, Peter and Mary-Rose O'Grady, Dave Owen, John Owens, Johnny Pring, RE Prout, N Raposo, Philippe Do Rosaria, Barry Sheldon, Andrew Sheppard, Marian Smith, Margaret Taylor, Lilia Teixeira, Tony Titchener, Bjorn Wahlin and Ylva Svensson, Haydn Walker, Henry Warren and family, Eve Watkins-Buskirk.

Photo credits

All images © Rough Guides except the following:

p.2 Praia Dona Ana © Terry Williams/Getty Images
p.23 The interior of São Lourenço © Hans Georg Roth/Corbis
p.25 Mediterranean Chameleon © Hans Dieter Brandi/Corbis
p.26 Lisbon to Dakar rally © Masarulho/Alamy
p.28 Surfer on Arrifana beach © PulpFoto/Alamy
p.29 Surfers on Praia do Tonel beach © Cro Magnon/Alamy
p.30 Zoo Marine © Malcolm Thornton/Alamy
p.34 Boat trip up the Guadiana © Matthew Hancock

p.35 Dolphin watching at Vilamoura © Matthew Hancock
p.37 Alcoutim © Matthew Hancock
p. 37 Alte © Matthew Hancock
p.37 Salir © Matthew Hancock
p.38 Mãe Soberana © Cro Magnon
p. 39 Coral Beer © Martin Siepmann/Alamy
p. 39 Festa de Populares © John Van Hasselt/Corbis
p.39 Sardine Festival © Owen Franken/Corbis
p.39 Almond blossom © Mark E Gibson/Corbis
p.48 Algarve town scene © Peter M Wilson/Axiom

Index

Maps are marked in colour

INDEX